100 WAYS TO BE A $HITTY SALESPERSON

Acknowledgments

Three people helped me write this book. heir ideas, wisdom, and encouragement have produced this (shitty) book. But it's shitty because I'm still a shitty writer. That said, the imputes to write wouldn't have happened without their impact in my life. If you want to be a shitty salesperson, don't look for people who can make you better.

Don "The Idea Guy" Holiday

- I met Don at Jeffrey Gitomer's Gitomer Certified Advisor Training. Don said a few things that have kept me awake for more nights than I can count. One thing hit hard, and I paraphrase: "You need the courage to look at old problems in ways other people haven't, won't, or can't." Most days, Don challenges me through his "Big Yellow Sticky" posts on Facebook and his newsletter.
  Don, thank you.

Jeffrey Gitomer

- On more than one occasion Jeffrey said, "writing leads to wealth." For 14 years I thought that "wealth" meant money. It doesn't. The wealth of writing is clarity of thought and courage of expression. You can't buy that happiness, discomfort, and drive to push forward. Jeffrey's Sales Caffeine can help you wake up to these lessons. go to: www.gitomer.com/sales-caffeine/
  Jeffrey, thank you.

James Altucher

- I started reading James blog and LinkedIn posts a few years ago. His book "Choose Yourself" is a must-read for anyone who feels trapped or who believes they can do more with who they are and what they've got. James once wrote, "Everyone has one good book in them." I don't think this is my "good book," but if you don't start writing, you'll never write *your* good book. Maybe your "good book" doesn't end up on paper, maybe it's a podcast, a *vlog,* or the way you live your life. All you must do is start and commit to getting 1% better every day. James' material is available on a variety of platforms.

Google him. He's easy to find and difficult to accept.
James, thank you.

DEDICATIONS

To: My wife who likes to say: "At least you're not afraid to admit your faults."

To: My Kids who've said: "Daddy, you're the best!" (at least I sold someone...)

To: My Probable Purchasers & Customers:

I'm sorry for being so shitty.

To: The managers who fired me: Thank you.

To Salespeople: Please be better than me.

CONTENTS

FORWARD

No sales book solves most of your sales problems. Why? Because "winning" or "success" is a unique experience. Said another way: doing right is particular; doing wrong is universal. No matter your situation, if you embrace any of these shitty ideas, attitudes, or behaviors, you'll be a shitty salesperson.

This book is hard to describe. It's sarcastic but honest. It's repetitive but fresh. It's common sense but nuanced. In those ways, it seems to reflect the entire sales process. The business of sales is difficult, peculiar, and confusing. I've read a lot of "sales development" books, and one thing rings true for 99%: While the advice might be objectively good, the specifics of your experience render the content irrelevant at-best, and at worst, destructive.

That doesn't mean you won't sit atop the President's Club or that you won't get the big bonus or be promoted to sales manager. You can do all those things and still be a shitty salesperson. Your status as a salesperson is not based only on your numbers. I've known plenty of people who couldn't make quota to save their life - but their honesty, integrity, and empathy for their customers made them great salespeople. These people struggled to get probable purchasers to say "Yes!" Conversely, I've watched may top performers leave shitty trails of destruction wherever they went.

I've often been a shitty salesperson who hasn't hit his numbers; therefore, this book is a critique of my attitudes, beliefs, thoughts, and actions. Dare I say, that's where I get my authority? I know one thing: mistakes. Twenty years of making the same sales mistakes caused me to miss bonuses, be put on probation, and get fired. If you want to make mistakes and be a shitty salesperson, this book is for you! It's a step-by-step guide on how to have a very painful sales career. It's my story. But I don't think I'm alone.

Another way to look at this book is through the lens of a cautionary tale or a mirror you can use to view yourself, how you think, feel, and operate. The choice is yours.

To find value in this book, you need to ask yourself: am I making the same mistakes as Nick? If the answer is "Yes!" then you need to find the reason. 99% of the time it starts with you – your attitude, ability, or effort. Once you identify your problem, take that problem (with possible solutions) to your manager and customer. Put it out on the table, don't hide anything, and be brutally honest about what happened and how you thikn you should fix it.

I don't pretend to offer any solutions or answers. If you are in sales and wonder why things don't "feel right" or you're struggling to get the next bonus or even keep your job, there's probably a relatable chapter. I don't know how to fix your problems, and I won't pretend I do. Fixing your problems is your business. This book is an outline of what mistakes to make to be a shitty salesperson, and if you read between the lines, you might find out a way or two to not be shitty.

Perhaps I might sound arrogant, but it's true: if you want to be a shitty salesperson, don't read this book. Tell yourself it doesn't speak to you. Tell your coworkers you're not guilty of any of these sins. Tell your boss that your numbers speak for themselves. Tell your customer's you'd never put your needs ahead of theirs. Then watch the reactions – spoiler: they're the reactions of people who deal with a shitty salesperson – you!

LIE, LIE, LIE, LIE, LIE

Shitty Nick learned to lie early and often. Shitty Nick got so good at lying that not only did his professional life become a lie, but his personal life followed suit. Days started with lies, at lies for lunch, and Shitty Nick went to bed lying.

If you become a pathological liar, you don't need to read any other chapters in this book. When you lie, big or small, for a short time or over an extended period, you destroy your credibility. But done right and you'll sound great! You own the narrative. Who cares if credibility sells? Belief in you, your message, and your ability to execute an action that primarily benefits your wallet is your goal.

With those thoughts as the foundation, there's one obvious question: is lying **really** that bad? No! Sometimes you need to "fake it 'til you make it" right? Sometimes it's best to fudge the truth because the ends justify the means. In most sales situations aren't life and death. Your professional career has almost no impact on the world. Life will barrel on whether you win the business or not. Say what you need to be believed and trusted – just enough to get the sale.

At first, lying will make you feel uneasy and leave a bitter taste in your mouth, but don't worry! Lying permeates everything, you do. Over time you'll build consistency and comfort with it. Sure, some bitterness will always mingle with the sweetness of your commission check, but that's OK - you got paid!

If you're reading this book, you're in sales, and if you're in sales, you've lied to get the deal. If you want to be a truly shitty salesperson, lying must be the cornerstone of your business.

Think of that time you inflated your commission numbers to get a job. Or what about that time you reported that you made more calls or stops than actual? Or that time you fudged your resume to say you made the President's Club when there was no way to verify? Or that time when you exaggerated a weak relationship? Or, or, or, or, or! Take 2 minutes right now and examine all the lies you make every day to make yourself more important, accomplished, and relevant than you are.

There's a direct correlation between being a great liar and a shitty salesperson. And if you can lie all about that stuff, can't you lie about product performance? Your team? Terms? History? Customers? It's a limitless resource.

Some might even argue that lying is an indispensable sales tool and that the more you lie, the more business you can win. Then when you get caught in the lie, if you play it right, you can make people think that you made a bad decision or that there were pressures that were outside of your control, and they might even give you a second chance. And really, are bosses ever upset when you have a contract? Not if it helps them get their bonus!

Lying can give you a leg-up over the competition. Lying can make your coworkers look worse than you. Lying can build a firewall around your other failures. Lying can be the difference between you and the commission check – so get comfortable with it, and you'll get the sale. It's your Trump card, and it only needs to work enough for you to get paid.

Need some places to start? Try these three:

- Lie your customer
- Lie your manager
- Lie to yourself

How do you lie to your customer? The best one is by not having expectations and experiences match up. Some people say it's best to under promise and over deliver or over promise and over deliver. To be shitty, you don't want to be accurate. Accuracy requires truth. Truth is the enemy of the shitty salesperson. Accuracy leads to tough, honest conversations. Your goal isn't to be accurate. Your goal is to get prospects to sign on the dotted line and press hard because there are three copies.

Lie about pricing because pricing is something that you can always fudge and move around based on what the customer buys or certain market constraints ("oh, inputs got more expensive..."). It gives you the flexibility to change price on a whim. Don't be afraid to lie about the terms. You can always say, "Management came out with something new. I know you're signing today, but this one provision that you thought was okay has changed, but we've gone far enough. It'll be all right." Lying about the terms is a great way to shield yourself and to make everybody else look bad because do you have any say in the terms? Of course not. Management is always changing the terms so you can't be held responsible.

Lie to your manager. Lie about the number of calls you make. Lie about how well meetings went or didn't go. Lie to sandbag. Lie about what customers say about your products, services, and pricing. When you start making up these lies, you can position yourself as the victim. If you're the victim, how can you be responsible for the current state of sales? You can't. Lie about what engineering told you so then you can get an inter-departmental fight that slows down the sales process which you can use as an excuse for not making quota.

Some issues are beyond your control; exploit them! Lie about market conditions and about what people are telling you. Make things sound much worse than they really are or much better than they ever could be. The lynchpin of a good lie is to never put the lie down on paper. That way, if the boss ever comes back and says something different, you can say, "Well, no. You agreed to X, Y, or Z" and there's nothing to dispute the claim.

Finally, lie to yourself. George Costanza said, "It's not a lie if you believe it." The great thing about the human mind is that you can convince yourself of anything. Once you convince yourself of something and believe it wholeheartedly, it might as well be true. It doesn't matter if you're a good team player or not – tell yourself you are, and actions be damned. Tell the world you're an expert – if you believe it, won't they follow? Demand high-profile accounts by puffing-up your qualification. Who is your manager to argue? If you believe it, it's true, and isn't your truth the only truth that matters?

Lie about everything. Don't fool yourself into believing you can get away with lying about only A, B, and C. Lie from A to Z. The result is no lie: you'll be a shitty salesperson.

PERFUNCTORY SALES

Shitty Nick quickly learned that if he checked certain boxes, even if he didn't always check the quota box, his manager would tolerate Shitty Nick's lack of production long enough for Shitty Nick to find a new job.

Take out a sheet of paper and put "Good" and "Great" on an X-axis. Then on the Y-axis, put "Minimum" and "Maximum."

If you want to be a shitty sales person, live in Quadrant Four. That way you'll never have to deal with the tension inherent to the effort necessary to go from *good to great.*

Nothing is ever perfect but if you set the bar at "good enough" then you might barely clear it. On the other hand, if you aim for perfect, sweat the small stuff, mind the details - put in the effort to make it as good as possible with the goal of perfection, then when you have 98.5% of what the customer wants at a price they can accept, you've positioned yourself to get the sale. But who wants all that work?! Why get 100% of what you need for 100% effort when you can get 80% of what you need for 50% effort?

Take shortcuts. Cut corners. Do the bare minimum because your reward for doing all that extra work will be more work. Or worse – no work! Have you known the salesperson who crushed quota year after year, and then they get handed a smaller territory and a bigger target. What kind of "thank you" is that? It's not! It's recognition by management that the salesperson is dangerous, and the salesperson needs to be fired or given such a painful situation that they leave on their terms (bonus for management: no severance or unemployment benefits).

You want to be just good enough not to be fired. Putting all that unnecessary and dangerous pressure on yourself isn't good for your business or your health. I've coined this behavior: perfunctory sales. You check all the boxes to avoid any criticism for not doing your job, but you never check any more than you have to – because that's dumb. Time is better spent at the bar, golfing, or gambling.

Take up Perfunctory Sales, and you'll check only the boxes you need to be a shitty salesperson.

ALWAYS BE CLOSING

Shitty Nick laughed his head off when he saw *Glengarry Glen Ross* because it depicted exactly what he felt he was and could be. If you haven't seen the movie, watch the opening scene 10 times. Why? Because as a shitty salesperson, one thing should always be on your mind: **A**lways **B**e **C**losing **(ABC)**.

It's a simple fact: people *love to be sold.* Nothing is more empowering to a buyer than being told that they've been closed. Use the worse "close" as much as possible. Make the close the most important activity in your day. Every sales discussion should be about closing. Always ask closing questions. Always force people to make decisions. Always brag about what business you've closed. Always highlight your closes to your customers. Always make sure your boss is aware of your most recent closes. Always talk to your coworkers about how much you've closed. Always tell everyone about how awesome you are at closing. They'll be so happy for you.

Don't you *love* that feeling of being closed? Don't you get excited when you feel that tinge of regret because you're not sure you made the right purchase, but you believed the salesperson more than your research, data, intuition, and experience?

Doesn't it feel gerat to know your salesperson is back at the office high-fiving their coworkers about how they got you to agree to X terms at Y price?

What's most exciting, as a buyer, is to see your name in the newspaper or online or talked about at networking events about how Joe Bag-of-Donuts "closed" on you and what a great deal that was for him and his company. Isn't all media good media?

You're wasting time if you think in terms of "a meeting of the minds" or mutually earned trust. The last thing you want to do is to talk to prospects and customers about new opportunities, partnerships, and collaboration. Don't waste your breath explaining about how "you'll be there for them" or that in working with you they'll have a concierge level of service. That will force them to *think*; you want them to *buy*.

Customers love being closed because spending money is empowering. If they work for a company, then they're not even really spending their own money. They're spending somebody else's money. Do they ultimately care if it works out or not? No way. They can always go and get another job. There's no risk to them. Every minute not spent closing is a minute wasted. You don't have time to grow and develop relationships. You don't have time to help other people out. You don't have time to put somebody else's needs first. You have a quota, crush it!!!

It's a huge mistake to send customers a hand-written (or at least signed) thank-you note after a purchase. Never give them a "post-purchase process document" that outlines how they can maximize their purchase. There's no need to check-in with them a month after purchase - that's the point of Account Managers and Customer Service teams! Those activities take away from additional closing opportunities! And since nobody ever sends referrals, don't bother asking for one.

The only thing that matters, the only thing that your sales manager or your owner is going to ask you at the end of the day is, "What did you do for me today?" Translation: "What did you sell ***for me today***?" It doesn't matter if you say, "I learned a new technique today that will help me tomorrow." Or "I helped John sign his deal today because he was struggling." Or "I worked with ACME, who bought from us three years ago, and even though they're not buying for another two years, I helped them work through a problem with our widget." Or "I reached out to 10 previous customers to see how they're doing." Or "I put out a free webinar for some prospects." If you're not closing, you're dying.

Can't you see why it's important to **Always Be Closing**? Get that cup of coffee; you earned it. As you chug down the Folgers, relish in the fact that you've mastered a great skill and are closing in on becoming a shitty salesperson.

REFUSE COACHING

Shitty Nick hated sales training and despised sales coaches. He never believed that with a little 3rd-party advice he could avoid a sales life of missed quotas, broken relationships, wasted opportunities, and light paychecks. He had better things to do: call, meet, close, and go to the bar.

Truth: you know it all. There's not a sales lesson you haven't learned, let alone mastered. What can someone 25 years your senior or (gasps!) 5 years your junior tell *you* about sales? They don't know what wars you've fought. They don't know your experiences. What wisdom could they possibly pass on? And if they are so good, why don't they do your job?!

Coaching usually causes four things to happen. Count how many help you close.

1) **The admission you don't know everything**
- Doesn't that give you the chills? You're an expert. You know all the features and benefits. You know how to make small talk. You know how to execute AIDA, ABC, FOMO, and FUD. You got hired, what's there to learn?
2) **You might have to practice something new**
- Who has time to practice something new? There's a quota to meet, a product to sell, and a prospect to close! Isn't all that training stuff a bunch of crap that doesn't apply to your business.
3) **Practice means longer work days**
- What a ridiculous idea! You read "The 4 Hour Work Week." You know it's all about working smarter not harder, and the thought of missing out on happy hour is a non-starter.
4) **Practice reveals secondary deficiencies**
- You can't possibly be expected to be perfect at everything. You know what you're good at and know that you should focus on your strengths and ignore your weak-

nesses. Why try to fix the few things that you haven't completely mastered?

Then there's potentially the weirdest event ever: your customer educates you! But how can that be? Aren't you the super-duper-problem-solver-extraordinaire? If you show yourself to be weak, your customer might not want to work with you. If you look at it that way, doesn't coaching sound self-defeating?

What happens after you've learned a lesson? You might have to show some humility. What's one virtue that has no place in sales? Humility. No successful salesperson ever confidently said, "That's an issue I've never heard of, I have no idea how that will affect your organization." You can't ever to having a prospect/customer issue you can't solve with the most elementary of solutions. No! Be bold, take your shot, and stand by your answer. Your confidence can make up for all your inability.

Don't listen to sales teachers or gurus. You're a pretty smart person and know how the world works. Your work speaks for itself. If that's the price a shitty salesperson must pay, it's worth every red cent.

LOVE BOILERPLATES

Shitty Nick became so good at memorizing his sales pitch, that even after a night (and early morning) at the bar, Nick could perfectly go through all the motions of a sales meeting at 8 AM. Shitty Nick never prepared, why would he?

Customers don't need or want customization – it's a completely foreign idea. Most customers face the same problems: losing money, not making enough, inefficiencies, blah blah blah. Why go through the trouble of tweaking and customizing if the customer only cares about price?

Because presentations are something salespeople are expected to "do," and customers never go back to check facts or validate claims, customization wastes time — a sales activity from a bygone era.

Think of all the time you will save by giving the same presentation ad-nauseam. You won't have to do homework. Customers only care about price, so get through the presentation as fast as you can, vomit a 20% price premium, tell them you'll see if you can negotiate, and voila - you'll close'm!

You won't have to take the time to go back to previous prospects and find out what they liked (or didn't) about your presentation. Why would you go back to them? They didn't buy from you. They're idiots. They've missed out on how you could change their world.

The first time you build a presentation and then present it, that's the best it will ever be – raw, unrefined, and bold. It's not wine so don't expect it to get better with time. Drone on, highlight features and benefits and get back to pricing. Next stop: Happy Hour!

Never take your prospect through a live demonstration - think of all the things that can go wrong! Test-drives are for suckers. Free trials are for wimps. Don't give your customer control or confidence. What will they do next? Ask harder questions and compare you to the competition! That sounds horrible, rife with pitfalls, and lots of opportunities for them to choose someone else.

Why go through the effort of a creative performance if the only thing that matters is the price? Why make them laugh? Or think? Or challenge an assumption? They don't want to do that! And who are you to offer such an outrageous experience?!

When you combine a boilerplate presentation with robotic mechanics, you'll sit in your safe-zone. Nobody will feel uncomfortable. Most people will thank you for your very informative presentation, take your packet, happily walk you to the door, and magnanimously shake your hand as they tell you "they'll be in touch." If your presentation has the right price, the customer will call and ask for a proposal.

Wash, rinse, and repeat the same performance over and over, and you'll set the perfect example of a shitty salesperson.

BASH THE COMPETITION

Shitty Nick believed that bashing the competition made him look good. Pointing out the competition's problems and deficiencies helped the prospect understand Shitty Nick and respond in-kind.

Want to make the other guy look bad? Follow these steps:

1. *Make broad-sweeping statements about the competitor's company*
   This step allows you to discredit the competition out-of-hand. You can drop innuendo. You can point out negative news stories. You can fudge historical data. The harder the information is to verify, the better for you!
2. *Embellish what competitions' customers say about the competition*
   You want to twist or distort facts. You want to give the customer the (false) *real* scoop. Ad hominem attacks are sure to paint your competition in a bad light AND infuriate your buyer
3. *Highlight the Negative*
   Whenever possible, whatever is good or legitimate, make bad. The more obnoxious you are about this, the better
4. *Highlight Past Purchase Mistakes*
   If your prospect has bought from the competition, be sure to highlight the terrible mistake they made. The more guilt and shame you can bring to the prospect, the better!
5. *Make stuff up*
   Nothing beats making stuff up. Go for the outlandish and the unproven. WIll the prospect check your claims? If it even sounds believable, it might be enough for the prospect to disengage and settle with you.

The best part about bashing the competition is that it reveals your true colors. It lets the prospect know who you are, where you stand, and what's important to you.

In short, by making other people look bad, you'll further your journey on becoming a shitty salesperson.

SEND THIS TERRIBLE EMAIL

Shitty Nick was an early adopter of technology. Email was in its infancy, and while his older coworkers sent faxes, Nick saw the power of mass communication. Copy, paste, send. Mail merges. BCC. Shitty Nick mastered the art of SPAM and if you're willing to ignore laws and general societal niceties about communication, you can do it too!

Email marketing evolved, but it's still the same process and one that's easy to exploit. What's the recipe?

- Make up an excuse
- Fudge details
- Use buzzwords
- Create a "call to action"
- Send, send, send!

You've probably never sent an Email or done a campaign like this, so here's a sample you can copy, paste, and format to your needs. The best part? With the right technology you can blast out astoundingly impersonal, incredibly vague, and rarely relevant to the receiver's situation without doing much more work!

What does this Email look like? Here's an example!

"Subject: Before Tuesday's Meeting

Hi Bob!

I've been trying to reach you by phone, but I haven't had the chance to catch you, you must be ***very*** *busy! You don't know me, but we do have a few things in common, and that might be a good place to start talking about business. I just wanted to reach out to you to talk to you about how I can help your business save money and keep people safe - you don't want people dying on you, am I right?*

Here at ACME we specialize in helping companies:

- *Be prepared for emergencies*

- *Get people in a position to react properly*
- *Organize data*

I know, as the health and safety person at your company, these issues are all top-of-mind because all the people I've talked with that are just like you tell me so.

It'd be great if we could sit down for 30 minutes and talk about some of the things you're doing and how we can help you do them better. In one meeting I know that you'll be happy to partner with us.

So I'll book us for a 1-hour meeting on Monday afternoon, we can go over all the details, and you'll be prepared on Tuesday. I really look forward to helping you implement our products. Please call me with any details."

You can create an Email just like this, pull together a mail merge, and automate sends weekly. Send the Email to everyone on your contact list – you never know who can refer you to the real decision maker. You're sure to get a response from someone – engagement! You'll also show a big list of "activities" in your CRM, and hit at least "3 of the 12 touches buyers need to have before they buy." Modify the Email slightly for everyone who doesn't respond, wash, rinse, and repeat.

Do you know what the words "SPAM" and "SHIT" have in common? They're both four letters, and so's another word that people will think when they see this Email from you, the consummate shitty salesperson.

IGNORE TIME

Shitty Nick shows no partiality when it comes to ignoring his time, his manager's time, or his customer's time.

Time should mean nothing to you. There's always tomorrow. Unless you get fired. Then it's just a different tomorrow. And you've got more time!

But what does it mean to ignore time? It means to ignore the difference between important and urgent. It means to procrastinate whenever possible. It means disrespecting other peoples' time, ignoring commitments, and putting your wants/desires over your customer's needs and requirements. How do you pull this trick off? Don't have a schedule.

One day, roll into work at 9:15 AM. The next, be there at 8:45 AM, *sharp!* Another day waltz in at 7:30 AM and send an email asking: "where is everyone?" Whatever you do, don't tell anyone your schedule – but if you need to, give them a vague ballpark. "Well, I hope to make it by 8:15 AM tomorrow, we can talk about the Pensky file at 8:30 AM." Now you've set expectations you don't intend to make and at the same time, disrespect another person's most valuable resource. But you know what? They can wait for you; you're the salesperson.

Traveling on business? Make it as convenient for you and if possible, as inconvenient for your customer, but more importantly: your company. They only abuse you and your time. Why should you set a standard of punctuality you have no intention of meeting? Why show prospects that their time is important when you know they don't feel the same about your time? How many times does your manager tell you to come back later or a prospect tell you to call back later? As if you have the time for that!

In the sales process, you have many opportunities to set the tone about time so set your time as prime time. Where does the sale start? It starts with you. Where does it end? With you. Whose time is most valuable? Yours. Business doesn't happen without you, so when you're ready to close – that's the best time. If you let customers and management control your time, you won't have time to make cold calls, send Emails, respond to proposals, do meetings, close, or go to the bar.

Follow these steps, and in no time, you'll be a shitty salesperson.

MASTURBATE

Shitty Nick loved sales masturbation. His mind ran wild with excitement as he approached the climax of the sale and then whether he won or lost, he walked away feeling good. Maybe not always with a contract, but certainly never any guilt.

A masturbatory sale is the pinnacle of self-gratifying and personally entertaining sales experience. What does this type of behavior include?

- A know-it-all attitude about the customer
- A presentation that's about you
- Solutions that reward you
- Terms that are in your favor
- Zero questions answered
- Unfounded assumptions
- Bashing the competition
- Absent-mindedness
- Inattention to detail
- ... and so much more

You've probably picked up on these activities in other chapters, but when you combine them all, the result is one of pure, unadulterated self-gratification. You feel good because you won. You feel good because the competition lost. You feel good because you got paid. You feel good because you got the customer to sign on the dotted line. You feel good because you got accolades. You feel good because you got a bonus. You feel good because you did whatever it took to get the sale. You feel good because you pushed your pleasure buttons.

In short, you got your orgasm, that's all that matters.

How do you get here? With a little self-exploration and experimentation. One of the best ways is to tell a little white lie. You can do this to your customer, manager, support staff, team, and even yourself. See how your customer reacts and the arousal of certain emotions. If the lie works, you will tingle a little bit from the excitement of "getting away with it." Then, as time goes on, feel free to tell additional lies - the rush you'll feel as you see people believe anything you say is almost unparalleled.

Next, put on the best show you can muster – without caring. Perform for your gratification. Really get into it - but by "it" you don't mean "solving the problem" you mean talking about how awesome you are. List all the customer's you've helped. Rip on the competition. Highlight every way that the customer loses by not working with you. Finish by telling them how stupid it could be to pick anyone but you. Tell them things like "You won't regret working with me!" and "If I were you, I'd sure pick me." Anything in that vein is sure to arouse a grandiose feeling of entitlement.

Finally, do whatever you can to finish the deal. Make up false timelines. Offer terms that can't be guaranteed. Give customers the "horse head." Don't think about how this deal might hurt the customer. Don't worry if you know they won't get stellar results. Remember, post-sale, it's the Account Manager's problem, not your problem. This moment is about you and your ability to **A**lways **B**e **C**losing! Work towards the climax the so you can and bask in the glow of a signed contract and self-pleasure. Don't care for your customer's needs - this is all about you and how awesome you are because you got them to say "Yes!"

Follow these steps, and you'll realize that nothing beats the feeling a shitty salesperson gets from masturbatory sales.

DON'T WORRY ABOUT THE COMPETITION

Shitty Nick didn't have the luxury to worry about the competition. The competition didn't focus on him, so why should he focus on them?

Name one good thing that could result in knowing your competition inside and out. Sales isn't a soccer game; it's a track race. You've got your lane; the competition has their lane. You do what you do; they do what they do. Simple. If you were crazy enough to research the competition, how would you do it and what would you try to learn?

What good could learning about an existing relationship do for you? How could you benefit by identifying the particular "ins" or advantages your competition has over you? You already know the competition's pricing scheme, right? Even if you didn't, how would that help you? It's THEIR price! Or terms? What good could come from understanding the competition's pricing and terms when your pricing and terms limit you? Aren't you the customer's best option? Why care about the competition? No control = no worry.

How could it help to know what questions the competition will ask? You've got your questions to ask! How could it help to know what the competition will say about you? Surely it's a lie! Your competition uses the same engagement strategies as you, what's there to research? Customers only buy on price so all this malarkey on how to "box" the competitor in or help the customer define *their* value proposition, so the competition can't ask deeper, relevant questions, is a fool's errand.

The bottom line is that every minute you spend researching the competition is a minute not spent closing. And isn't that what you're supposed to do? Close, close, close!

Don't research the competition and nobody will have to research to find out if you're a shitty salesperson.

KNOW IT ALL

Shitty Nick knew it all. That's what he was paid to do. Memorize features and benefits, quote a price, get a signature, and move-on.

Is that any different from you? Isn't that why management pays you? You can learn any product. You've attended relationship building seminars. You know how to network. You know how to spend your time. You know how to talk to customers. You know how to take notes. You know how to write deals. You know how to negotiate. You know how to present. You know how to close. You know how to build bridges. You know how to make connections. You know how to get referrals. You know how to beat the competition. If there is anything to know in sales, you know it. You know it better than anyone. You also know this book isn't for you.

What else do you know?

- A "no" today is also a "no" tomorrow so why build a long-term relationship today?
- Selling on pain is the best way to sell.
- People love to be sold.
- Fear is the salesperson's best tool.
- There's nothing to learn from losing.
- Belief is more important than action.
- Customers only buy on price.
- If you're not cheating, you're not trying.
- Honesty is often the worst policy.
- There's no value in not immediately answering a question.
- It's ridiculous to ask for further explanation, more details, and greater insight.
- You waste time when trying to understand nuance or detail.
- There's no reason to slow down a transaction.
- Having a thorough database is a way for manage-

ment to put undue pressure on you.
- Getting the sale is always better than not getting the sale.

You know that to be a shitty salesperson it means to know it all, all the time, and to put it on display for everyone to see.

HOLD ONTO LOST SALES

Shitty Nick reveled in yesterday's lost sales. He would use them as an excuse for under-performing today. Nothing quite motivates a person more than dwelling on the past, right?

Letting loose your feelings of anger and resentment feels good. Sharing your misery with your manager, team members, support staff, current customers, family, and friends is an inalienable right of salespeople. Those people love hearing about how stupid the customer was for not buying from you. You can see it in their eyes.

Bosses, family, friends – they all nod and say things like "Oh yah, I totally understand" and "Look, it sounds like you did everything perfectly, I can't understand why they wouldn't buy from you!" Getting that feedback is great because it shows you what you've known all along: you're right.

Remembering past failures in the heat of the sales moment is exhilarating. You can draw upon past mistakes to raise your level of anxiety which makes you perform worse (stress /= success), and the customer will undoubtedly sense your nervousness and even fear of losing the sale. But don't you have the right to be nervous? You can't be expected to answer *all* their questions on the spot, right?

Lost sales give you a lot to talk about with your manager. Going into an internal meeting or review without any failures is a dumb idea. You need to give your manager something to work with. If you could highlight a handful of failures but exaggerate your efforts, you'll almost always get at least six months of probation to "right the ship" instead of one quarter. Those six months are important; you can use the time to improve (falsify) your resume for the next job.

Pine over lost sales as you throw down another beer or take a hit off the joint. The prospect didn't deserve your service. They'll come crawling back, they always do.

And a final piece of advice - if you've got real courage, you'll make sure to make some remark on LinkedIn or other industry message board about the mistake the customer made by not going with you - that'll really stick it to them, and you'll be that much closer to earning your badge as a shitty salesperson.

OBSESS OVER YOUR COMPETITION

Shitty Nick was a bit of a conundrum. He either spent no time worrying about the competition or all the time worrying about the competition. The competition would boil his blood because Shitty Nick could never figure out what they were up to and why he always lost. But worrying about the competition did do three things for Shitty Nick and you can pick up right where he left off. What goals can you accomplish if you constantly worry about the competition?

1. You feed your *Excuse Machine*
2. You increase your level of paranoia
3. You paralyze your decision-making process

The first goal you'll achieve is the feeding of your Excuse Machine. To be a shitty salesperson, you've got to have a healthy Excuse Machine. The Excuse Machine will give you the fodder to rebuff any advances of customers and management. When you're worried about your competition, you spend a lot of time thinking about what they are doing and spend no time worrying about what you need to do.

You'll be able to highlight to your manager the competition's superior features and benefits. You can use those "facts" to pick apart why you didn't get the sale. It's not *your* fault you didn't have the inside track that they did. It's not *your* fault management sets the price. It's not *your* fault that the terms you've got to march with don't fit with your customer's business. See how wonderful this is? You get to shirk responsibility and make a case why you should get another shot (not be fired).

Next, you'll increase your level of personal and professional paranoia. You should revel in paranoia. Nothing makes you feel more alive than when you're worried - especially about things you can't control. The great thing about your paranoia is that you can project it onto other people. Your lack of comfort, preparation, and expertise can be felt by your customer, coworkers, and managers.

Once customers feel your paranoia, they can relate to you. They will begin to doubt their intuition and expertise. Deficiencies are great because you can use them to lower the cusomter's expectations and you end up not looking so pathetic. All you're doing is changing the lens they view you through to help you not stand out, to dampen your contemptible behavior, and to make your paranoid behavior not be so extreme because you've increased their paranoia. It's a wonderfully vicious circle.
The final goal of worrying about your competition, is analysis paralysis. If you can't make a decision, can you make the wrong one? No way! What do you do with your indecisiveness? You use that to spread the blame onto other people! You ask everyone how to handle an objection, and then you take someone's advice and do that and when you're asked: "why did you do that?" you say: "Bob told me to!"

You can also play the "damned if you do, damned if you don't" card which is incredibly powerful. "I'm sorry Boss, I didn't drop the price because then we wouldn't make any money." "I'm sorry Ms. Customer, had I gotten those terms agreed to, you could sue us for non-performance." "I'm sorry Support Staff, had I made the copies and bound the presentations; I couldn't have gone to that networking event."

So, feed your *Excuse Machine*, embrace paranoia, and don't make any decisions - all effects of worrying about your competition.

Do those three things, and you'll never have to worry about being a shitty salesperson.

DON'T KNOW WHEN TO QUIT

Shitty Nick never knew when to quit. He kept on, pursuing to the next block, would bust a left and cold call the next stop, and if the prospect was dead, yo? He'd continue to a1a, Deadbeat Avenue!

Listen to your manager at all costs. Keep smiling and keep dialing. Ask the same customer over and over and over if they want to buy from you. Extract every resource you possibly can from your support staff. Push your team to do more and more for you and give them less and less.

Quitting is for losers. Who wins a war by quitting? Sales is all-out war. A war between you and the competition. You and your manager. You and your customer. You Never quit; especially if you experience the following:

1. Your sales manager or boss tells you to do something illegal or unethical. They made the call; you're not responsible, just do it.
2. When your customer asks you too much of your time that your personal life and other professional relationships suffer.
3. Boredom with your job. Boredom means you're an expert!
4. Your company stinks. Each industry needs (and has) a few dogs - this is your opportunity to be the "low-cost alternative."
5. The competition keeps winning - don't worry, it'll turn around someday...
6. If your company stops investing in you. Those dollars meant for your improvement can go towards making better products for your customers which will result in easier sales for you!!!
7. When your company makes it harder for you to succeed by upping your quota and shrinking your territory - they're just helping you stay focused!

When the going gets tough, the tough need to get going! Quitting means you've got to start over, learn something new, and be forced to grow. In my opinion, better to be miserable and secure than happy and insecure. At least you get to collect your salary before the whole company goes under, right?

If you can remain in the dark about when to quit, you'll never quit being a shitty salesperson.

SELL LIKE A CHILD

Shitty Nick threw the best sales temper-tantrums. He would yell at his boss. Cry to his customer. Pout in front of his support staff.

Nobody ever wants to grow up, so why should you? Be a child. Be green. Be immature. People always give kids a second chance so why not you?

How do you sell like a child? Yell, scream, and demand. The childish salesperson demands everything from the buyer and offers very little in return. Easy enough.

Children often sell through temper tantrums. Make enough of a scene, and you might get the customer to do anything to make you shut up. Contract signed, check cashed.

You can also cry - metaphorically and literally. Just start blubbering in front of your customer or on the phone. Tell them how much you need this sale. Tell them that you're going to lose your job, that the mortgage won't get paid, that your spouse will leave you, kids will hate you and nobody will respect you. Play that sympathy card!

Don't worry about any trail of destruction you'll leave for the next salesperson who will take your place - that's their problem, not yours.

Don't accept decisions if they don't make you immediately happy. Lie to get what you want. Withhold value until you get something first. Keep things to yourself, be moody, don't share insights and advice with other coworkers. Be very afraid of rejection. Act like Shitty Nick did in high school and college (not just as a child) and avoid rejection all together!

Keep your mind closed. There's one way to do things, and that's your way. No need to experiment and explore - you know what works.

Still confused about how to do this? Watch children play for 20 minutes. Take note of all the ways they manipulate people to get what they want. Watch how people react to their tantrums.

If you can make customers buy from you to shut you up, you'll grow up to be a shitty salesperson.

IGNORE THE SALES VIRTUES: 1 OF 4 – WISDOM

Shitty Nick was a big believer in the "wis" part of *Wisdom.*

3,000 years ago, Greek philosophers laid out the Four Cardinal Virtues: wisdom, justice, temperance, and courage. Some might argue that they're also the "Four Sales Virtues." Do you think they ever had to make quota? But if you've got a quota to make, so ignore these virtues, and you'll have something else to focus on.

What is sales wisdom (or prudence?). Simply put, it's the acquisition and proper application of knowledge. Whoa, heavy. Wisdom sounds like a lot of work. But there are three things you can do to enjoy the bliss of ignorance: waste time, waste assets, and waste relationships.

Wasting time is a great way to stay ignorant. Watch more TV. Spend more time at happy hour. Play games on your phone. Show up late. Leave early. Try to multitask. All these ways are great tactics to waste time and remain ignorant. You've got lots of assets at your disposal. Product demonstrations, videos, marketing content, and business social media. Whatever you've got access to, either overuse or don't use them. Don't bother striking a balance. You can't possibly thread the needle of a varied mix of engagement assets, can you? That would require a lot of learning, practicing, and experimenting. You'll spend a lot of time evaluating your process, and you might get it wrong! Doesn't sound like "closing" to me.

"Relationship" is just a word for "care." And can you honestly care about your customers? They only care about your price. What good is a good relationship with your manager? Managers only care about your closing percentage. What's the big deal about having a good relationship with your coworkers? Coworkers only care that you're closing, so they have a paycheck. Relationships are just a means to an end. The only question that needs answering is: what does this person mean to me?

There's no excuse for you if you've got wisdom and still don't do the right thing. But if you remain foolish and ignorant, it's nothing but bliss. Remember Cypher and *The Matrix.* You want the blue pill.

You don't have the time to practice, be thoughtful, and get guidance. Shitty salespeople are ignorant - and ignorance is bliss.

IGNORE THE SALES VIRTUES: 2 OF 4 - JUSTICE

Shitty Nick **just** didn't have enough time for *Justice.*

What's justice and what in the world does it have to do with sales and is there any such thing as a "just" sale? That's one long and stupid question. Justice is in the eye of the beholder. You can't possibly expect someone to agree with you on what is *just* and what is not. What is *fair* and what is not. What is *equitable* and what is not.

But if you were to be *just* or employ *justice*, it would mean that you'd have some identifiable guiding principle you'd rely on to make small and big decisions. In sales, do you have that luxury? No! Look at your job description. What does it say about business ethics? Fair treatment of customer? Personal integrity? Nothing! Aren't those traits incongruent with getting the sale? As a salesperson, it's your job to get people to sign on the dotted line and worry about any "problems" later.

Here's a simple equation: If the sale doesn't benefit you, then it's unjust. Think about it... if you can't sell or if the sale is unjust to you, how long will you try and sell it? That's why you've got to be the main beneficiary of the sale. Without you winning, nobody else can, right? The price needs to benefit you so that you can stay in business. The terms need to benefit you and your company so the customer can't pin you down over some minor technicality. And don't worry about your *personal brand:* that's an illusion and something you can change by changing companies.

Think about the costs associated with being a just a salesperson? First, you've got examine how you think, learn, and act. Exhausting! Then you should go to a 3rd Party so they can give you an honest critique. 100% painful and what do they know? When's the last time they walked in your shoes? When selling, you must ensure that both you and the customer win, but your boss doesn't care if your customer wins, only if you close the deal. And if you don't get the sale, you'll have to rely on *courage* when you go back to the customer and find out why you lost. Can you go to your boss and say: "I had to pull this deal, the customer was going to lose out in the long-run"? Have fun with that conversation.

And what if you are *just*... how does that help you? What if justice means a smaller commission? What if justice means no referral because the customer finds out your products and services don't meet their needs. Can you really turn *justice* into actual money? Could you charge more for being *just, fair, reliable, transparent,* and *honest*? Good luck! Maybe that helps your brand, but can a good brand help you beat your quota? No way, customers only care about price.

Just sales? Not in my experience. Don't ask those deep philosophical and theoretical questions that could impact your day-to-day workings. They're immaterial. Customers care about price more than whether or not you're just and fair in dealing with them.

Ignore justice, and you'll be on your way to being just another shitty salesperson.

IGNORE THE SALES VIRTUES: 3 of 4 - COURAGE

Shitty Nick had enough courage to make the required amount of cold calls – what more courage do you need?

Most people know the phrase: "There's a fine line between courage and stupidity..." but most don't know that it's a two-part quote that continues: "...If you get away with it, you are courageous. If you don't, you are stupid." Look, if you fail, you're stupid. You weren't smart enough to say the right things to get the customer to buy from you. And your real stupidity sits in the fact that you didn't realize how stupid the customer is and you didn't take advantage of that stupidity.

Some people say we're born with courage and base that on our "fight or flight" instinct. Isn't that cavalier? If courage is a virtue, then we need to learn it and learning takes work, and that work takes away from cold calling and closing. What boss tells you they want you to be courageous? What manager demands that you take risks? Trust me; they'd much rather you sell and ensure their bonuses than take a real chance at something and risk their plush vacation.

But let's say that you decide to pick up the mantle of courage, what then? A lot more work. If you've got courage, you've also got to build your ability to be merciful, vigilant, faithful, and hospitable - even when people are jerks to you. How can any of these virtues help you on a cold call. In what world does that work?!

Courage means that you've got to do the right thing, even when nobody is looking. Here's your choice: do the wrong thing and pay your mortgage or do the right thing and not. What will you do? That's simple math.

Courage forces you to stand-up for people even when it's not your battle. Why should you put your neck out on the line for support staff that has screwed up or a customer who's not had their expectations met? As a shitty salesperson, your job is to oversell and get the customer to believe whatever you say. If you've got courage, you're going to have to admit your mistakes and as you've read elsewhere in this book: **shitty salespeople don't admit mistakes.** Admitting a mistake gets you fired - dumb!

Courage puts you in the position of doing things other people can't or won't. You must speak up when you see injustice. You're required to highlight product deficiencies. You're forced to have to tell your manager that your product/service is not the best for the customer. You're compelled to spend more time trying to do what's right than doing what makes you and your company money. Where's the cash in that? It's in the competition's pocket!

Shitty salespeople don't have time for courage because they know that the shots they don't take, they don't miss.

IGNORE THE SALES VIRTUES: 4 of 4 - TEMPERANCE

Shitty Nick had to take care of himself. He knew that if he won, everything was OK. And if the customer struggled? Maybe they didn't have the temperance to endure a shitty salesperson.

What's temperance? It's a component of altruism, which consists of helping others, sacrificing your well-being, receiving no external reward, and acting voluntarily. Can you imagine something more antithetical to sales? It's the exact opposite of sales. If anything could be defined as "not sales" then "temperance" would be it!

To have temperance means to have self-control. There's no room for self-control in sales. You are a hunter. You eat what you kill. You kill whatever you want. Why should you ever show any self-restraint? You push pain buttons as much as you possibly can. You want your customer to feel uncomfortable. They've become numb to their pain. It's your job to get prospects to feel their pain. Remind prospects, as often as possible, about how much pain they are in. Any restraint you show will slow the sale – not good when you've got a quota to beat.

Speaking of restraint, have you ever seen "restraint" in a sales job description or talked at all about by any manager. Restraint is for the weak and feeble. Restraint requires some sobriety of thought and nuance of language. I've got no time for that. My job is all about AIDA:

Attention. Interest. Decision. Action.

That's the order and done as fast as possible so customers can't think about what you're saying. As soon as prospects think, actions slow, questions are asked, objections are raised, and commissions are delayed.

Temperance is a methodical way of doing business that requires moderation. That's all degrees of crazy. The sale is about you and what you do to get customers to buy. You're here to put it all out on the line, plain-as-day obvious as possible, and without any need to soften my tone. You don't have the luxury of reconciling self-control with self-promotion, restraint with aggressiveness, and moderation with maximizing shareholder value.

Temperate means a laser-focus on the quality of the result, not just the signature on the dotted line. The former activity, that's the realm of the Account Manager and Customer Service team. Being temperate requires you to ask tough questions about who wins, when, where, and why? As you read about in the *Courage* chapter: only if *you win* can anyone else win. Do you have the courage to embrace that attitude? Temperance raises questions about personal and brand legacy. We will all die, and so will companies; screw your legacy and get your commission check.

Temperance might be the culmination of all the other virtues that allow you to properly respond to everything the customer might throw at you, but if you want to be a shitty salesperson, be intemperate with temperance.

DON'T BE HUMBLE

Shitty Nick loved to use humility, thankfully it never taught him how to be humble.

There's absolutely no room for humility in sales. And you need to rid yourself of any humility if you don't want to succumb to any of the sales virtues.

Have you been wronged, cheated, passed-over, treated unfairly, humiliated, or marginalized? Have you been released or had your position terminated or even fired under less-than-fair circumstances? Have you been relegated to activities below your intellect and capability and watched those who objectively provide "lesser value" usurp you due to office politics, incompetence or ignorance? Has your boss or customer made you the scapegoat when something hasn't worked out? Of course! The world is cruel and unless you're willing to return it with equal cruelty, you will to continue to beat by the next sales guy.

Stop being humble. You live once. It's *you* or *them.* There's no room for turning the other cheek: you've got a product to sell and a quota to hit.

Here are three steps to avoiding humility:

1) Never own up to what's right in their critique of you

When someone says you've done something wrong, you need to turn it around and put that wrong on them. Did you miss quota? It's because your manager didn't give you the right tools. Did you not earn the sale? It's because the customer is stupid. Did you not deliver the best presentation? It's because marketing failed to support you. All of this is easy to do and can easily stop you from being humble about what happened, taking responsibility, and offering some restitution for your errors...oops, *their* errors.

2) Never accept that you've wronged other people

Reality: you never do anything questionable because you're trying to get the sale. You've been told to do whatever it takes to get the business...or you're fired. If you miss quota, is marketing fired? Does customer service get demoted? No! You can do no wrong as a salesperson so long as you come back with a signed contract. If a customer says you've short-changed them, cheated them of an opportunity, or denied them a place they're trying to claim as their own – forget them. You do what you need to do to get the sale.

3) Forget forgiving and forgetting

Who has time for this attitude? Someone screws you, screw them back - especially if they caused you to lose a sale. They've got to feel the pain of their mistake otherwise they'll never learn! You've got to remind them of how many times they've screwed up and made it harder for you to get the stupid customer to say "yes!" If you can do this publicly - in front of your peers and managers, all the better. Show them that you know what's right and how you got screwed. Do that frequently enough, and it's only a matter of time before that never happens again!

Being humble, lowly, and meek are poor ways to be a sale professional. Grab some arrogance, promote yourself, and have the sales world revolve around you and you'll be a shining example of a shitty salesperson.

NEVER ASK THESE THREE QUESTIONS

Shitty Nick never asked these questions, and the result? He always got the answers he deserved.

What am/will I be known for?

We're all going to die, so who cares about your brand. To remembered, you've got to pick an important discipline, like putting out maximum effort, always looking for opportunity, or being diligent about partnerships. Are these virtues great? Maybe, but do they help you cold call? How can they help you find the pain? Do they drive the customer towards AIDA? Can you count your brand like you count your money? This is a Rubik's Cube puzzle, so don't waste your efforts on it.

Why do I want to be here today?

Since when has "why?" mattered? Isn't paying your mortgage motive enough to show up for your job every day? This is such a stupid existential question. You're at your job because you need to be. Nobody will work for you. Aren't all the other "benefits" fluff? Can you make the world a better place? Can you solve a problem for a customer? Is it possible for you to help them "win?" Isn't it a pretty rare experience for a customer to come back and thank you for all your efforts in helping them buy a product? Do you need a deeper meaning than your paycheck?

What am I doing today to be here tomorrow?

Here's what you're doing: your cold calling and closing. And if you don't close as much as possible today, then you won't be here tomorrow. Keep that "professional development" crap in the box. Think expanding your horizons can help you beat quota? Show me. Think having a "good attitude" can get you on the boss' "good" side so you're not fired? All my bosses loved me. I still got fired six times. Sell or be sold - give questions like these to philosophers.

Self-reflection is a painstaking skill that takes time to develop.

It's like a daily job interview. It's the one thing you must do if you want to be bigger than you are. But I'll tell you this, asking these questions will put up a big roadblock on your path to becoming a shitty salesperson.

MAKE YOUR INTERNAL SALES MEETINGS STINK

It was never Shitty Nick's fault that his sales meetings stunk.

Sales meetings are excuses for your manager to talk about how awesome he is and how crappy you are. Managers laud their favorite salespeople (even if they're not the best) and rag on you because you haven't closed enough. They ask stupid questions like "what worked last week" and "tell me about an objection you couldn't overcome." Then he will try to be the "Knight in Shining Armor" and ask you what deals you can bring him in on... the nerve!

It's not easy to make a sales meeting stink, but that doesn't mean you can't

1) Never take the lead
Look at all the things you must do every day to keep your job. You don't have time to lead a sales meeting. Don't try to set the agenda. Don't try to outline things that are important before the meeting. Don't take ownership. The meeting is clearly for the sales manager to show their importance. Let the manager talk about what he wants to - you stay calm, cool, collected, and most important: quiet. You need to worry about your own upcoming sales meeting and how you're going to get the customer to sign on the dotted line. Running meetings isn't your skillset, and it's a non-transferrable skill. If you've never been asked to lead a meeting, it's because you're obviously better suited for other tasks.

2) Be quiet
Sit quietly. Mimic your manager's non-verbal signals (like nodding/shaking your head). Avoid eye contact by looking "beyond" your manager. Squint your eyes and rub your chin to make it look like you're thinking. If called on, just say "I've got some ideas I need to flesh-out, keep going, that might help." See what that does? You look like you care, but you gave your manager a reason to continue and forget about you. The last thing

you want to do is offer up an idea - unless of course, it's a frustration. If something stinks or isn't perfect, bring it up and talk about it passionately. But don't be merciful. Be highly critical and share examples of how it's hurt you personally. Whatever you do, don't offer solutions; that's the manager's job.

3) Don't critique yourself
Everybody wants to hear about how good you are, contracts you've won, and how much customers love you. Exaggerate the health of your pipeline and throw out phrases like "My opportunity list is about to push hard into my lead list - going to crush it!" Never share your struggles because you're the BSD. You're not paid to talk about your mistakes, and any mistakes you reveal could be used by your internal competitors (your co-workers) to sell against you.

Sales meetings are unhelpful time-wasters. They never add to your bottom line. Follow these three steps, and you're sure to be a shitty salesperson.

MAKE YOUR EXTERNAL SALES MEETINGS STINK

Shitty Nick never believed it was his job to make an external sales meeting awesome. He was there as a favor to the prospect and you could smell it on him.

Intentionally making a sales meeting bad may seem like a no-brainer, but it's much more critical than it appears on the surface so here's an outline on how to screw up a sales meeting.

It can't be stressed enough: don't prepare. And really, what is there to prepare? If you know the features, benefits, terms, and pricing of your product or service, isn't it up to the customer to figure out if what you've got is right for her?

Next, show zero interest in figuring out their motives. If they were honest and wanted your help, wouldn't they tell you? Why should you have to dig? Just throw out the classic reasons why people buy your product; you're bound to push some pain buttons .

While presenting, show no passion for your product. Could your excitement transfer over to your customer as he debates between you and the competition? Probably not. So what if you deeply care and believe in your product, isn't that what you're paid to do? No need to go above and beyond the minimum requirements, it's not like the customer buys you first and then your product... Save your passion for your football team.

Don't do any homework. What you learn about your customer is irrelevant; at least as it relates to the price of your product. Plus, if you do homework, you might find areas where your product or service is inadequate for her needs. Is that a situation you want to be in? Let her figure out you're not good enough. What benefit could showing your deficiencies bring to the table? When has honesty ever won a deal?

Only focus on the material ROI. How much money does your product save your customer? Do whatever you can to inflate that number. Most people only buy on price so there's no point in trying to sell the Mercedes when the Oldsmobile will do the job.

Make your customer ask all the questions. Don't challenge any of their assumptions. And remember, you must always be professional. Forget fun, light-heartedness, and laughter. They're certainly not interested in the personal side of business. Better to always be prim and proper than cool and comfortable.

Finally, never ask for the sale. If you don't ask, you will avoid making the customer think about your product. Remember, if you don't ask, you don't get (rejection!).

Take this very robotic and predictable approach, and at the end of the meeting, she will thank you for a great presentation. As you walk out the door without a signed contract, you can make all sorts of promises to follow-up and in the process follow through on becoming a shitty salesperson.

SELL LIKE WELLS FARGO - 2000-2016

Shitty Nick never liked sales training, but after reading about the practices at Wells Fargo, that's a training program he would have aced.

I'm not picking on Wells Fargo. Heck, I'm still a customer, but the behavior from the top on down to the front lines couldn't be a more perfect example, and it makes me wish I had actively employed their strategies instead of just stumbling onto them by accident. And while most of these things were driven by management, that doesn't mean you, the front-line salesperson, can't start them on your own.

First, set unrealistic expectations. Everyone should have a goal that's nearly impossible to meet, that way they will always feel pressure to do more, even when doing more isn't the best thing to do. Is a reasonable quota ten deals a month? Set the quota at 20 and just watch how you (or your team) behaves. First place: a Cadillac. Second place: steak knives. Third place: you're fired.

Second, take the "Office Space" approach to selling by asking, "Is this good for the company?" This question is code for "Does this activity drive profitability?" If the answer is "yes" then do it. Cross-sell, up-sell, bundle, and never ask questions like "Is this good for the customer?" or "Could this possibly damage the trust between us?" We're all going to die, you'll get fired, or he will move on; what's the big deal? Be the "Company Man" and reap the rewards.

Third, focus on the lifetime value of the customer and try to extract it as fast as possible. This step builds on the second because it's here that you can start doing some of the more *aggressive* things that can drive commission:

- Offer products customers don't need
- Hide secret renewal terms deep in the contract
- Force them to sign by selling on FUD/FOMO before

customers can do research
- Bill customers for services they don't want or need and let the Account Management team deal with "misunderstandings"

These behaviors embodied the Wells Fargo sales culture for over a decade - and it worked! Wells became the biggest retail banker in the world. Who cares if the banker opened a few dozen unauthorized checking or savings accounts? Or if people received credit cards that caused them to live beyond their means? Maybe the customer needed the credit?! These behaviors were just the salespeople doing what was best for the company... and doesn't the company write the paycheck? Sure, it resulted in some fines, but not before Wells was able to make a ton of money, pay the fines, and have a surplus to pay themselves huge bonuses. Perfection, no?

If you want to be a shitty salesperson, follow the Wells Fargo model, and you'll have no problem writing checks your body can't cash, you Maverick!

SELL LIKE DONALD TRUMP

Shitty Nick had a mentor; he didn't know him or use him, but he's pretty sure Donald would be one manager who wouldn't fire him.

Donald Trump is the shittiest salesperson, but look at him, he's a billionaire... and president! If he can do it, so can you. It starts with attitude, encompasses process, and results in you having the image of the quintessential shitty salesperson.

How do you sell like Donald Trump? Be a big, fast-talking chameleon focused on your commission check. Remember: the costs of getting the sale are inconsequential to your commission. You'll leave a trail of destruction in your path and somehow, someway keep your job, be lauded as a great leader, and might even get promoted!

Be the bully to post the biggest number. You'll drive fear into your peers and managers. If you're the major revenue driver for your company, who's going to stop you? Who's going to stand up to you? Nobody. You're the CEO without the title or responsibility. You'll be allowed humiliate and abuse customers and staff. So long as you get the sale, you're untouchable.

If you make every sale about you, your win, and your commission, you'll be just like Trump. In the most extreme cases, you can even bankrupt a company, but you'll get your check and stand a good chance at getting another swing with another company. It's sick, twisted, and demented - but it works!

Pander to the audience. Appeal to their most base instincts. FUD and FOMO are your greatest assets. They can push even the most level-headed customer into a decision they know is not in their best interest - and you get paid! Rile them up with overblown statements. Bash the competition. Tell them exactly what they want (not need) to hear.

You want to be high on expectations and low in detail. If you tell people they will win over and over again, many will believe it. All you need are enough people and attempts to make a career out of it. Promise as much as you can and leave it to other people to execute. And once you ink the deal, take all the credit for it. Your support staff is there to support you, and they should be thankful for the money you make so they get paid.

Finally, never examine your behavior. There's no point. Your job is about making sales. Nobody's paying you to be a better person. There's no bonus for evolving. The rewards are only felt *by you* and in *your wallet.*

If you want to be a shitty salesperson, sell like Donald Trump - who knows, maybe you too can be president!

USE THESE WORDS

Shitty Nick had a sales vocabulary 10x of his average commission check. Be like Shitty Nick and soon you'll be a wordsmith of shitty salesmanship.

Leads and prospects. That's what people are. Don't you like being considered a lead or prospect? They're words that can dramatically impact your personal and business relationships. You must avoid more technical terms that put value behind people; like the term "Probable Purchaser." Ignore the fact that people are on a journey and they live on a buying continuum. Once you give someone the title as *Probable Purchaser*, you've got to do things like qualify and quantify how close they are to buying and buying from you and worse: if what you're selling is good for them! That's not closing, and closing is what you're paid to do, so forget it. Want a few more gems?

Closing. Speaking of closing, use this word around customers as much as possible. People love to be closed. It brings out warm and fuzzy feelings of uneasiness, manipulation, and doubt.

Cheap. Always talk about how cheap your product is - especially relative to the competition. People love cheap stuff. Avoid words like "inexpensive" and "minimal investment." Those are just frilly words that don't let people judge your quality like they can with the word "cheap." Cheap means a deal and a deal is what they want, so talk about cheap!

Hope. Hope is a word a politician uses because (s)he doesn't want to take responsibility for failure. Tell customers what they can hope for by buying from you. It's also a great way to oversell without making promises you can't keep. Need more?

- **Honestly**: If you say "honestly" it implies that you're vulenrable, the prospect can feel that vulnerability and appreciate it. Truthfully, you should always use honestly because honestly and truthfully are ultimately filler words that leave a customer believing you would never lie to them, honestly. Plus, when you use honestly/truthfully, it makes you sound genuine. See how genuine that sentence read (if not, say it out loud)?

- **Follow-up**. Always tell the buyer that you'll follow-up. They want to know that you're going to come back. What are you going to come back with? It doesn't matter; they only want the attention. They want their phone to ring so they can feel important. A bonus would be giving something they need...but what you're more interested in is another one of your "12 touches necessary for a person to say yes." A really simply way to kill two birds with one stone.
- **Account**. Nothing says: "you're just a number" more than the word "account." If you tell customers that they're an *account*, then you instantly put a dollar value in front of the relationship. Tell customers that you love "servicing their account" because when you do that, you remove the personal aspect of your relationship. Stop calling people customers or clients - they know what they are: a number on your way to your bonus. Treat them as such.
- **I've called/I'm Calling**. Always start a conversation with these words. If you're looking for great pointless words that stunt your opening and hamstring the rest of the call, these are guaranteed to work.
- **Presentation**. If you're buying, do you want to watch a presentation or a performance? Do you want to see a robot in action, or do you want to see passion? I thought so... you want to see features, benefits, and price. Actors perform – you're a salesperson: you present! I can't count the number of times prospects told me how good my presentations were and how professional I was. Not that those comments turned into signed contracts, but they sure loved me presenting – they said so every time!
- **Price**. It always comes down to price, so use that word.

If you use a word like "investment", then you must quantify things like ROI. And really, what's a good ROI? Is it ever good enough? Let the customer decide; you tell them the price. "Cost" is equally a powerful as price.

- **Today**: Very few salespeople have businesses or sell products that require people to buy today but that doesn't mean you can't treat people like today is the most important day in the world to be sold. *Today* exudes FUD and FOMO, so tell customers "If you sign **today**, we can do X but if you don't sign **today**, well then, it's not nearly as **cheap**!" You don't want the customer to feel like they have control over the situation. You're the salesperson; you're in charge, they do what you want to do when you want to do it. Today's the best day to sell and for customers to be sold - so treat it with that way.
- **Commission**. Always talk about your commission. Tell customers what you make, how much you make, and where you make it. Let them see where the real cost of their purchase. They want to know that they're buying from a member of the President's Club. They'll send a bottle of wine and chocolate to your room for your bonus vacation. Not that that's happened to me - I've never made the President's Club, but I'm sure you will if you talk a lot about your commission to your customer.
- **Quota**. Want to get the sale? Just tell the customer "I really need you to buy **today**, so I can hit my **quota**, can you sign right now?" Maybe you've done well this month, tell the customer "Can you hold off on your signature so this deal counts for my next quarter's numbers?" Nothing says you care more about yourself than talking about your quota with your customer. They know it. They know you care more about your commission than anything else, and they know that if you win, then they might win, and you might be around next year when they need to buy again. Share your quota numbers with customers - it's your only sympathy card, so play it!

These are the words of a shitty salesperson – use them, love them, live them!

QUESTIONS TO NEVER ASK A BUYER

Shitty Nick hated questions. He was in the "answer" business. Shitty Nick gave answers prospects wanted to hear. But if you don't know what questions to avoid, how can you be like Shitty Nick?

What if? Which are? When would? Who can? When do? What could? Where would? Why not?

Everyone talks about "power questions" - well, there they are. But asking those questions can make people feel vulnerable, and the only way they're going to answer those questions is if you make them feel safe.

Making people feel safe in a transaction isn't your job. You must sell on FOMO and FUD; not making people feel secure. Prospects don't want to share their motive, so don't invite it. Do you think prospects want to tell you that the only reason you're in the room is that they screwed up and need to fix something, fast? Or that their last supplier dropped the ball and an immediate solution is needed? When's the last time a prospect told you about a new project or initiative and their need for your products and services? Prospects don't share that information because they know if they do, you get to raise the price!

If you start down the road of asking things like "what if?" and "why not?" expect some complicated answers, even expect that they don't have the answer. That only means more work for you. These questions promote dialogue and trust between the parties - both artificial constructs used to make business relationships seem more important than they are. Sure, they *might* be buying questions, but you're going to have to go back to your team, ask a lot of questions (the correct way), then get the answers back to the customer, and then maybe adjust your price higher (harder to get the sale) or lower (less money in your pocket).

It's incredibly tempting to ask these open-ended questions that get prospects to think, but you don't want them to think. Are you really prepared to respond to the answers these questions demand?

- What if? This is an opportunity question, it requires more follow-up, and creativity on your part.
- Which are? This question couches roadblocks and forces you to solve problems.
- When would? This is progress question – you don't need to know progress, you need a sale.
- Who can? This question forces the person in front of you to admit that they're not the ultimate decision maker and shows you how far you are from the sale. Scary.
- When do? This is a timing question that can show you how much more work you must do to get the sale.
- What could? This is another opportunity/roadblock question. The only valid one is "What could I do to get you to sign today?"
- Where would? This question demonstrates your willingness to go above and beyond. Why would you do that? Your commission is set. Do the bare minimum.
- Why not? This question starts the removal of your favorable terms and pricing.

Do prospects buy because they want to or because they must? That answer doesn't really matter. It's obvious that when you start these probing questions that cause prospects to take a step back and think about what the purchase means, it usually means more work for you which drops your overall hourly rate and often your total commission, because answering these questions fully and honestly wastes time.

If you want to be a shitty salesperson, don't ask these questions and enjoy the fact that you'll never have to provide an answer.

SEND PROPOSALS

Shitty Nick loathed proposals. Why does the prospect need all this extra information? Shitty Nick told them the product worked and the price. If the customer only cares about the solution and price, isn't the rest of it just a waste of time? You know why prospects ask for proposals? Because prospects want to feel important and like abusing sales people.

Reality: you got the meeting, puked your features/benefits/ price on the customer, and now you've been asked to get them a proposal – ugh! Why?!

Now you have a choice: send the proposal exactly as they asked for OR try to get a proposal meeting to go through how your product/service is the best solution.

Keep it simple, Email it. You've asked enough of the customer's time. Customers have other things to work on. This is exactly why someone invented Email. They're smart people. You can convey 110% of your value through images, graphs, and text. If they can't see the value, are they blind?

Think about what it would mean if you insisted on a proposal review meeting.

1) They'd have to agree to it
- which is just like another sale
- which will require more time
- which could slow down the process

2) You've got to do a *really* good job
- this takes away from other cold calling activities
- this bites into your social-hour sandwich
- you will be put on the spot again

3) You might experience rejection face-to-face
- you're not paid to get rejected, your company pays you to sell
- nobody bears the brunt of rejection more than you; you do it

enough
- better to be told "no" via Email or over the phone than face-to-face

Send the standard proposal. Don't risk creativity. Don't try to make your capabilities exceed the proposal requirements. Some might argue that this is a great place to add value. Isn't it really a great place to step in "it?" Taking this shot of trying to WOW your customer could end in total disaster, and there's no prize for second place. They want a proposal, they know what they need, who are you to question their assumptions?

Buyers love when sellers do exactly as they are told. If there's one thing to know about proposals, it's that if customers tell you how to be a shitty salesperson, you can do it, and they'll be happy.

DON'T WRITE

Shitty Nick hated reading, writing was even more ridiculous. Who has time to write when there's a call to meet, a meeting to do, and a contract to sign?

Writing is time-consuming, thought-provoking, and downright dangerous. When you start writing, something weird happens - you start to question everything you know. Is that something you really want to do? You know your product, industry, and customer base. You know what those groups want, the challenges they face, and how to deliver it. Perfectly, every single time. Why challenge it?

But when you write, the things you knew suddenly become unfamiliar. Things you took for granted are now hard to pin-down. Everything that was comfortable is now uncomfortable. It's weird, freaky, and uneasy.

Salespeople don't have time to write. Your job isn't to express your thoughts but to share a company vision for your customer. You're not a problem solver. Customers always know where the hole in the dam is, you're just selling the best widget to fill it.

As a writer, don't you have to care what other people think? Doesn't the reader's opinion matter? If so, why put pen to paper? You're putting yourself out there to be judged and rejected. Does that help you close? Does that bring credibility?

Writing demands responsibility. Gross. You must find feedback. You must learn what parts of your message resonated (and what didn't). You're required to go back to your "thought writing board" and dig down to find out what mistakes you made. Talk about a lot of work for clear thoughts and the ability to directly relate a message in a way that resonates with the reader! Most people can see a mistake, but it takes a ton of effort to find out *why* the mistake happened in the first place. It's exhausting.

And really, who's going to read what you write? Will, a customer, read an article you've written for a trade magazine or post on LinkedIn... or book? Pffft! They're busy watching TV just like you and worrying about all sorts of problems related to profitability, efficiency, disruption, and job security. Writing is an activity that forces you to think creatively, look at the world a different way, and finally put your thoughts out to the world and be judged. Does any of that highlight a feature or benefit? Does it explain how your terms are better than your competitor's? Nope!

Writing isn't easy. Just look at my ad-hoc list of all the things you need to do before you finally hit the "publish" button and put your neck out there for everyone to chop off:

1. Brainstorm. More like Shitstorm. It's Marketing's job to come up with the fancy ideas – not you!
2. Set a publication schedule. You've got calls to make, reports to turn in, meetings to hold, beer to drink, and TV to watch. There's not enough time.
3. Set a writing schedule. You've got to do it 10,000 times to become good, so you need a schedule, but read #2 again - you don't have the time!
4. Read similar topics. If you don't have time to write, you certainly don't have time to read. Heck, isn't it football season?
5. Compare/contrast. Are you regurgitating old ideas, or have you put out something new? That's homework. Yuck.
6. Engage customers. Yup, put your work out in front of them so they can judge and give another reason not to answer your Email or return your call.
7. Think about delivery. Do you Tweet? Instagram? Use LinkedIn? Post on Facebook? Write a long-form article that pulls apart the various pieces of your industry and offers an opportunity for you to write in how your product fits and try to place pieces in

these channels. That's not closing.

8. Think thematically. Building a narrative is super hard. Would Marketing or Communications help you? Probably not; that's their domain but not for you to use. Why are you stepping on it?
9. Be relevant. Look at the past, present, and conjecture about the future? One would have to be crazy to do that.
10. Edit. There are reasons you're a salesperson and not an English Teacher.

Do you see what you need to do to write? Do you understand how much time this takes? Can you comprehend the fact that you'll be putting yourself in the spotlight for judgement? What if a decision maker doesn't like the article you wrote? They might not answer your call/Email… let alone buy from you?!

You receive enough rejection as a salesperson; this is just another way to feel that pain. Embrace the fact that the cold call is mightier than the pen and you'll write yourself into the annals of the shitty salesperson history.

ABUSE TRAVEL

Shitty Nick loved getting out of the office and doing it on the company's dime. Want a step-by-step guide? Keep reading!

It's your life, your job, and your time. Do with it what you want. You never have to answer to anyone – epseically if you're hitting your quota. And even if you're not, aren't you *trying?* If your *Excuse Machine* is functioning correctly and you're comfortable with lying – abusing travel might be the easiest thing you do all year.

Schedule out of town meetings for mid-morning. This means you can avoid getting up at 5 AM to get on a 7 AM flight, landing at 9 AM and having to be sharp at 10 AM. You want to go the night before and *still schedule* that meeting for 10 or 11 AM. You can easily do this under the pretense not wanting to miss your meeting because of the flight, car rental issue, or some other avoidable incident. Better to be put on an afternoon flight on the previous day, right?

Highlight how you travel by using discount online booking tools, so the company gets the best deal. Now you've shown your *commitment to company profitability* while still working less to get paid more. This gives you a better chance at burying a travel schedule that primarily benefits you under things that are good for the company. If you're given a travel budget, always travel for 5-10% less than budget, and you'll have fewer eyes looking at your departure/arrival times.

If your manager is in a different city than you (best-case scenario), you can easily make up excuses about travel that are difficult to verify. Excuses can come in many forms, from airport construction to TSA delays, and even aircraft mechanical issues. Put all of this together, and you've got every excuse to build your itinerary around a schedule that fits your needs.

Sales managers like to tell salespeople "Your job with us is like your own little business." You know that's a big lie, but since it's a lie and disingenuous, treat it as such. Travel is a great way to stick it to your company because at every opportunity you can ensure you benefit. Managers can fire you, screw with your commission schedule, and make it harder for you to sell (easier for them to fire you). This is one area that you can push back without much impunity.

If you're looking for other time-sinks, one of the best is rental car pickup. Give yourself an extra hour of padding because that line is always long and there are very few ways to avoid waiting in line so if you think it'll take you 30 minutes, plan for an hour. When you travel, you're the one that's away from your spouse, kids, trivia nights, and bowling. Your manager isn't missing out on those opportunities, you are. Make them pay. The only thing that your boss misses out on is your delightful presence in the office.

Perhaps my best trick was never to schedule concurrent meetings on the same day. Follow that advice and it almost always guarantees a few days out of the office on your company's dime. How do you do this? First, puff-up the importance of the first customer. Say that you don't want to have to cut a meeting short if things are moving towards the close. How can your manager get upset about that?! Second, push the second customer to accept a late-afternoon meeting and then tell your boss that the only chance you can meet is at 4 PM. Is there a 7 pm flight you can jump on? Nope! You've got to wait 'til the next day. Aww shucks! Are you feeling gutsy? Schedule an 11 AM meeting that second day. Boom, you've just burned 2.5 work days, missed out on stupid meetings, and got to eat a few good meals on the boss.

These are just a few great ideas you can use to spend as much extra time traveling as possible. The best part? Traveling like this is a first-class ticket to becoming a shitty salesperson.

THE FIVE RULES OF CLOSING

Shitty Nick hated most rules. Other people put rules in place to keep you down. But Shitty Nick had five rules he relied on to *always be closing.* And customers loved it. He could watch the prospect react to his rules and it always sped the closing-process.

Rule #1 - Remember that people love to be closed
People love to be closed and if you can tell them they're being closed, all the better. They will feel relieved at being closed. They'll know where they are at in the process of saying "yes" and that will bring relief to the anxiety they feel while at your mercy.

Rule #2 - Always be direct about closing
At the end of every call, email, and meeting ask prospects: "Are you ready to buy yet?" And the word "yet" is the most important word to use because it tells them that you're ready and there's no need for them to wait any longer. The more arrogant of a tone you use, even one that's a bit insulting, the better.

Rule #3 - Ask the following questions:
1) Don't you love our product?
2) It's great working with us, right?
3) Where would you be without me?

These are all great closing questions because as soon as the prospect answers, you've closed the sale...

Rule #4 - Don't let prospects ask questions
You want to highlight features and benefits then immediately throw out the price and say, "Do you want to buy this?" If they have questions, tell them you'll get back to them, but to show you that they are serious, they need to sign on the dotted line. Everyone needs to have skin in the game, or the game can't be played fairly, right? Don't give oxygen to questions like "What if? Do we have to? Can this be changed? What happens in a year?" Those questions just the process and shrink your commission.

Rule #5 - Make prospects feel like they have no other choice
By using guilt, desperation, FOMO, and FUD you can always move closer to the decision. Make prospects feel like not buying from you is a huge mistake that puts their hopes, dreams, and job in jeopardy.
These questions show prospects that you're serious about selling (them) and their need to move forward with you immediately.

Hammer away at these questions, and you'll forge yourself into a shitty salesperson.

IGNORE MOTIVE

Shitty Nick had one motivation: earn a commission. If only the prospects recognized his motive for what it was, they would have made a better choice.

If you find the motivation for purchase, you have found the truth, and the truth often doesn't set you free. The truth will tell you what's wrong with *your* company, *your* service, *your* product, *your* pricing, and what's wrong with *you*. Motive is the number one reason people (don't) buy from you. If you find motive must meet or even exceed their standards to get their business. Said another way: you'll have to work more to get less.

What are possible motives?

- the problem they need to solve
- the pleasure they want to experience
- the type of person they like to work with

Motive drives the purchase and comes in a variety of forms - all of which often means more work for you. For some customers, it's an emergency purchase. For others it's strategic. Sometimes the motive is completely political... do you want to get involved in intra-office politics just to sell your product? Wouldn't it be nice to avoid all those fights and rejection?

Of course, you can't simply ask for their motive, right? As if a customer would tell you why they would want to buy something from you. That would give you all the power and help you shape your message to be most appealing to their needs and wants. Can you expect someone to be that open with you, to trust you that much? To rely on your expertise? How much time would you have to spend to build that kind of relationship? Probably way more time than you have – because you've got a quota to meet!

If you stumble onto the customer's motive, you might come

face-to-face with the reality that the motive doesn't match who you are or what you have to offer. Motive will tell you everything you (don't) want to hear. If you start hearing about things you don't want to hear you got decisions to make. You're forced to change. Change is hard, scary, and not always beneficial. Change involves reflection and risk. Change forces you to take responsibility. Is that the price you want to pay for finding a motive?

Is finding motive worth your 7% commission? Forget finding motive; it's incredibly dangerous and finding motive gives you power. Just stick with features, benefits, and pricing. That'll give you enough motivation to remain a shitty salesperson.

JUDGE A BOOK BY ITS COVER

Shitty Nick knew the value of judging a book by its cover. All you do is look at somebody and decide whether they deserve your product, can afford your product, and could become a great referral source for you and your product. One of the more enjoyable parts of this skill is that you can do it on so many different and offensive levels.

You can use racism or sexism. You can discriminate or judge the book by its cover based on socioeconomic position - it's always easy to tell who has money and who doesn't; who would be a profitable customer and who wouldn't. From the moment you lay eyes on a prospect, treat them how you think they deserve to be treated. If they look poor, treat them like they're poor. If they look rich, treat them like they're rich. If they look like they're from your clan, treat them like they're from your clan. If they don't look like they're from your tribe, treat them like they're not from your tribe.

Prejudgment is a great set of horse blinders. You don't have to listen to what prospects say or try to understand where they're coming from. You don't have to analyze any of their needs. You can make decisions about what they need and how you will sell them. Who are they to determine if your product is good or bad for them? That's the salesperson's job, and of course, your product is the best thing for them... today!

If you correctly prejudge the prospect, she will know exactly what you're doing and respond in kind. She'll appreciate your obtuse understanding of their position in this world. They might even tell their friends about how good of a job you did prejudging them and their needs without asking a lot of questions.

People appreciate being judged because it gives you that shortcut to know exactly who and what they are, what they believe, what they stand for, what they need, and why they should buy from you.

In the end, they will take the same shortcut and define you as a shitty salesperson; voila, you've reached your goal!

TALK YOURSELF OUT OF THE SALE

Shitty Nick was awesome at talking... and talking... and talking. Without knowing it, he became the best person to torpedo a deal. Since he was always in control of the sales process, it was like pulling strings to wreck a deal.

How do you talk yourself out of a sale?

First, tell the customer you're not the best solution – even if you are. This false meekness does wonders. If you want to make the prospect doubt you and your offerings, tell them that you're terrible. You really want to overplay your deficiencies and your shortcomings.

Second, be vague about their ROI. How? Highlight the lack of emotional, physical, financial, operational, cultural, or any other perceived and factual benefit about the product and services you represent.

Third, be opaque about the post-sale process. Say things like "What a wonderful question, and if we ever get to that situation, my team will be happy to help you work through it." Here you have said everything, but nothing substantive. Brilliant.

Fourth, tell your prospect why somebody else didn't buy and exaggerate reasons for why they didn't buy. If you can fabricate a story by using exaggeration and puffery and facts and nobody can verify the facts, you'll do a great job of talking yourself out of the sale.

Fifth, continue talking after they have said yes because this is going to open the door for doubt and skepticism to grow. Plus, you never know what stupid thing you'll say next – but the more you say, the stupider you can sound.

Finally, tell prospects why one of their competitors bought from you. That will stroke their ego and increase feelings of

competitiveness or bitterness towards their competition. Just watch what happens when you tell a probable purchaser why their competitor bought from you. The prospect's belief that their competitor is stupid, doesn't make the right decisions, and doesn't understand the competitive landscape, come together to tell the prospect that if their competitor bought from you, they should avoid making the same mistake!
As you think of the products and services you sell, can't you safely say there have been a handful of experiences where you knew the customer would buy, but because you kept yapping, they changed their mind?

If you want to be a shitty salesperson, keep talking. It's a surefire way to get you walking out the door without the contract signed.

BE COMFORTABLE

Shitty Nick was always comfortable. Shitty Nick viewed himself as a thoroughbred that needed to be fed, groomed, and massaged by his manager, team, and customer. And only when he had been treated so majestically would he even consider running the race. If Shitty Nick wasn't comfortable, everyone knew it - an easy thing for you to imitate!

Sales is hard work. It's grueling and painstaking. It takes every ounce of energy to be successful. To increase your odds of success, you want to be comfortable because comfort = wins. Think of yourself as an athlete, where if you're not comfortable in the right clothes, shoes, with the right team, then you're just not going to play well. It's so hard to overcome the discomfort that it's not worth your time.

Getting uncomfortable means doing things you're not used to, things that carry unknown risk or have a list of unknown unintended consequences. You need everything to be predictable. You want to know the end-result, otherwise, aren't you just wasting energy? If it's worked before, why won't it work now? If it hasn't worked before, why would it work now?

For instance, what if you're a non-technical person and need to get comfortable working with industrial manufacturers and engineers. What uncomfortable things might you do? First, get out of your office and visit their site to understand their process. You're not an engineer, never have been, never will be. How are you supposed to understand their process? Do they expect you to research their industry and show them insights as to how they could improve profitability and efficiency? The customer knows way more about their industry than you ever could, so try?

What next? What if they have a different political and social ethos than you? How can you be expected to work with someone who has such a backward view of labor and capital? They should be grateful you are willing to show them your software. Isn't it bad enough to deal with backward-thinking family members at Christmas, now you must do it to get paid?

The real kicker? They want details, lots and lots of details. Are you a detail person? What if they want you to explain every detail from how the software is installed, to dealing with legacy files, training, updating, add-on modules, and much more? Aren't your letters of recommendation about the product from people just like them good enough? Why do they need all these answers from you? Isn't that what sales engineers are for? No comfort, no fun.

What questions can you expect to answer? Try these on for size:

- What are the various properties, tinsel strengths, and costs of steel on the open market?
- How would their supply-chain be affected by more nuanced orders?
- Would I be able to use a newfound knowledge about how futures contracts worked for raw materials and the impact that had for the entire ecosystem they worked in?

You didn't go to college for that. Who has the time to do an online class, or read a book, or spend a day or three with customers trying to gain insights into their business? Not me! Not you! You've got to close!

Remember: the game of sales is a numbers game. Do more numbers, and you'll get more numbers. Can you become more knowledgeable... AND meet your quota? In all these years, Shitty Nick didn't. Why put in the effort? Find your groove. Find your stride. Let the chips fall.

You'll have a paycheck, and you'll have your job – said another way: enjoy the comfort of being a shitty salesperson.

SELL THE SIZZLE

Shitty Nick thought he was the Chef of Sales. He believed everyone wanted to eat at his restaurant because even though he couldn't make shit shine, he could make it smell good enough to buy.

Salespeople love this saying because it is a promise and an excuse in one dish. By selling the sizzle, you can say anything. If you stick with the food analogy, it means you can say you're using an exotic herb or spice – when you're using salt. It means you can talk about the quality and cut of beef – when you're using sirloin. Get the picture? It's about getting the customer excited about the prospects of perfection baked into an imperfect dish! And then you go and use whatever you want. Save a buck, charge more, profit on the margin!

Sell the excitement. Sell the dream. Sell the feeling. Abuse the reality that buyers first buy on emotion and then back it up with logic. If their stomach is full, do they care about how it tasted? No way. If it sounds good, smells good, and looks good, what's the difference if it's Wagyu or USDA Grade D? Why should the customer care what they get if it only matters what they think they got? Why would you tell them any different? The only thing that matters is their perception.

If prospects are happy through the process and believe your promises, do they have a right to be mad at the result? If you can make them think that what they are getting is great, they're going to say "Yes!" a lot faster than if you're completely transparent. To use a legal trick, use puffery. Exaggerate. Make borderline statements. They'll smell the success oozing from your lips.

What's the best way to sell the sizzle? Tell people exactly what they want to hear and nothing else. If they want to hear that your primary effect is saving them money, tell them you save them money. If it's that you make them money, tell them that you make them money. If it's that you make them more efficient, tell them that you make them more efficient. Reality-be-damned. Whatever they need to hear to sign on the dotted line is what you need to tell them. That's your role as the salesperson, getting signed contracts. Not helping, serving, or educating.

When prospects bite into that steak, and it's not what they thought, remember, it's their perception that's wrong. It's their mental and emotional taste buds, for lack of a better term, that are uneducated. If there's a post-sales problem, move the buyer to the customer service department. Let Account Management fix the dish. Your job was to get the sale; it's their job to keep it.

If you cook up your sales that way, you'll be a Chef of Shitty Sales.

DON'T PRACTICE

Shitty Nick knew that there's no such thing as "practicing sales." You do or do not. You can't afford to practice. If it works, great. If not, whatever. Call, meet, sign. What else is there?

Show up to your job at 8:30 AM. Make your calls. Do your meetings. Fill out your reports and always be closing. Go home at 5:00 PM. You don't have time to experiment. You don't have the luxury to identify 50 or 75 or even 100 accounts that you shouldn't sell to and to and try new ways of engaging probable purchasers. Why in the world would you want to practice a skill when you have a quota to meet? What could you find out by going back to purchasers who rejected you and asking them why you were rejected? What benefit could you get by asking them if you had tried a different avenue, could the result had been different? It wasn't you; it was the price. You already lost the sale, move on!

The ship sailed, what's the point? You don't have the luxury of A/B testing. That's an activity for the Marketing Department. What could you possibly learn by setting up a mock sales presentation with your existing customers? They're already your customers. Could they tell you something you don't know? They've told you enough - they bought once, they'll buy again.

You can't practice building relationships, finding common ground, or overcoming objections. You can't practice making cold calls – what if you screw up and they never take a call again? How do you practice time management? Don't even start with "objection management." The only objection is price.

Role-playing situations within your sales team are a waste of time and a total joke. Those events can't possibly reflect anything that you need out in the real world. Stick to the basics. Know your product. Know your features. Know your benefits. Know your final price.

If you know that much what else do you need? Even if you did practice, do you have the skill to transfer that information to an actual sales pitch? Are you motivated enough to watch yourself in a video recording or listen to a recorded presentation? Do you have the time to listen to somebody else's feedback when they've never walked in your shoes? Will people take your ideas seriously? If they do, aren't you improving your internal competition? That's a terrible idea!

People say: "practice makes perfect" *not* "makes quota."

The bottom line is you have a target to hit every month and every time you don't hit your target your job is on the line. You don't have the luxury to practice. Focus on making as many cold calls as you can and let the cards fall where they may. Take up this mantle, and you won't ever spend another hour practicing to be a shitty salesperson.

ONLY YOUR PERSPECTIVE MATTERS

Shitty Nick saw things one way: his way. His way was the right way and he believed it was OK for the prospect to not agree – they could take their business elsewhere.

There is only one point-of-view that matters in sales, and that is the viewpoint of the salesperson. Salespeople are the experts. Salespeople know everything. Salespeople must always be in control. Salespeople determine the truth. Salespeople define what is helpful. If you're about to stand in the shoes of your customer, then you're about to experience their pain, and struggles, and desires. Why would you want that? You know what they need, so tell them what they need.

You don't ever want to be in a position where you must accept the fact that your product, service, and company isn't in the probable purchaser's best interests. If you see things that way, the next thing you'll see is you missing your quota. Remember, you know that you and your company, and your products, and your services are the best. They're the best for everyone: all the time, for all things - your price is justified. You also know that because you engaged with the customer on the phone or in a meeting, that right now is the best time for them to buy!

There's no legitimate reason to wait. You're there to sell as much as you can in the shortest amount of time, even if what you sell doesn't meet the customer's needs. If you start seeing things from the customer's point-of-view, you might have to be satisfied with just a trial, or, God-forbid: having to give away something for free so they can experience what you, your product, and your company are all about before they have to say yes. Commission in jeopardy!!!

You never want to be in the position of seeing things from your customers perspective because (just) maybe, in a rare instance, what you offer is not in their best interests. But who cares about their interest? You have your interest: your commission. What happens if you go down that road?

Congratulations! You helped them make a great decision, but your wallet is the same size as it was yesterday. Take the position of superiority. Don't give an inch. Your perspective is the only perspective that matters. As a salesperson, your only job is to convince the prospect that what you've got is what they need (not *best,* not *appropriate,* not, *responsible*).

Don't be tempted by the illusion of enlightenment by seeing things their way; otherwise you'll risk being labeled as something other than a shitty salesperson.

PANIC!

Shitty Nick loved to panic. People could see his stress, frustration, and fear. When he was in a panic, people acted. Is there a better definition of "teamwork?"

When something goes wrong, panic. Don't breathe, assess, or think. Panic. If you have an hour to solve a problem, take immediate action. Don't look two or three moves ahead. Run around like a chicken with its head cut off. Let everyone experience your emergency and make yourself the priority.

How you operate under stress will tell your prospect everything they need to know about you. If you panic, they'll feel it and might even feel sorry for you. Customers love a volley of rash decisions and ideas because it shows that you're a person of action. Thoughtfulness? That's for HR. Creativity? That's for marketing. Details? That's for engineers. You are about action.

Make sure the customer hears the uneasiness in your voice as you walk them through the solution — stuttering and stammering work great. Filling silence with "umms" and "ahhs" sends powerful messages to customers. Avoid being methodical. Always be noncommittal. Don't say things like "I'm not stopping 'til I'm done." Rather, say "If this works, it'll be a miracle."

Customers like to hear lines like "When there's something to tell you, I'll tell you." "Just give me some time to work this though!" (try to sound annoyed). "What more do you want from me?" is a real winner. So is "I'm doing as much as I can!"

Never say the following:

- "We want to send our best people to you, so they can see what happened."
- "Here is the data we have on what went wrong, does that match your experience?"
- "I've got a working solution unless you disagree, can I begin the fix?"

- "Here's how we solved this problem for X, can we try it with you?"
- "I understand that this is going to cost you $X. We will give you a credit plus a discount on your next order, or cut you a check ASAP for your lost profit, that work?"
- "Once this gets fixed, and it will, you will get a post-mortem for you to review along with detailed steps about how this won't happen again."

If all of this seems like a lot to digest, follow this acronym:

P = Publicize the problem and blow it out of proportion
A = Avoid taking any responsibility for what happened
N = "Nickel-and-dime" on anything to do with money
I = Insinuate that the customer is the reason for the problem
C = Cost-out how much the fix costs your company and make your customer feel bad about it

Follow these steps, and instead of panicking about being a shitty salesperson, you can rest easy knowing you are one.

NOTHING FOR FREE

Shitty Nick hated giving something away for free. Customers want free meetings, free demos, and free trials. *Free* is a commitment-less relationship and if you start giving things away for free, it might stop you from being shitty.

You need a commitment from the customer. You want as much of their skin in the game as you can get away with. You want them feeling like their place at the table is special, if only fleeting. When you start giving things away to your customer, they will act like the character in the children's book "If You Give a Mouse a Cookie." In that book, you see exactly how all customers operate. First, you give the mouse a cookie, then the mouse wants milk, and before you know it, they've got the farm! That's how customers behave. They're abusers and will take everything from you they possibly can. You can't trust customers.

Reality: help costs money. Do you go to the doctor for free? Do you go to the bar for free? Lots of salespeople give away free consultations. Isn't that a load of crap? Charge prospects $100 for your time. That's going to tell you who's really interested because if they're willing to pay $100 they're probably willing to pay anything else. I have lost track as to how many times I've told customers that meeting with me would cost them $100 – nobody ever took the meeting, and I avoided wasting my time on tire-kickers.

You might say that people might want free trials. Well, then you'll have to invest with them to get their 30 or 60 or 90-day free trial. What do they do next? Complain about price. You've got to ask yourself: why do I sell? To help your customer or to make you money? Can you serve two masters? What profit can you gain by giving something away?

What if you give something away that requires implementation from your team which takes away resources from your other existing customers? It's a disaster. The truth is, whether you have the best or the worst product, if your price is low, you've got a shot. Why should anything be free?

Do you think giving something away could generate good-will towards you? Do you expect them to do something for you in return? Never happened to me. Then again, I stopped giving things away for free a long time ago. When you give something away for free, customers go behind your back and giggle about what an idiot you are. They smirk about how generous you're trying to be even though you've got no chance at the business. You're opening yourself up for abuse.

What if "free" gave your customer time to figure out what's wrong with your product? What if "free" gave your customer time to think about terms? What if "free" gave the customer time to highlight things that you could do differently? Does any of that guarantee a paycheck? No. The only thing that guarantees a paycheck is an exchange of money for goods and services.

Don't give anything away for free and you'll be free to become a shitty salesperson.

DON'T QUALIFY PROSPECTS

Shitty Nick knew that the process of qualifying customers always slowed down the decision process. If you've got a pipeline to fill, can you afford the time it takes to qualify a prospect?

Not qualifying prospects is wonderful because what you do by not qualifying prospects is artificially inflate the number of prospects (the top of your pipeline). You look like you've got lots of opportunities, you're always busy, and this can feed your *Excuse Machine* because lots of opportunities give you lots of excuses.

How are you supposed to know a lot about the customer? Things are always changing. Nothing is ever consistent in business. One day the prospect might be qualified, another day they aren't. Better to treat them all as qualified, wait until the end to get the truth, and let the numbers shake out as they do.

Who are you to qualify somebody? If they want to buy from you or could buy from you, who are you to say no? Your job is to sell your product or service and sell as much and as fast as possible. It shouldn't matter who is buying and it really shouldn't matter when they're buying. If they can buy, then they're a lead; they should all get fair and equitable treatment.

Rather than qualifying people, you should talk to them about how awesome your products are, how fabulous you are, and the great things that your company can do for them. Let them get the message. If they call in, jump right into your pitch. Worrying about their buying process is unnecessary. Who cares if they're a drain on your company's resources? That's Account Management's problem. And isn't it Engineering's job is to make stuff up out of thin air; help Engineering do that by signing anyone that wants to buy – no matter what they're asking for!

If they're talking to you, they're interested. Prospects qualify themselves. You need to figure out how much they can buy.

Timeframes, budgets, and critical business issues change. Trying to qualify someone is an exercise in futility. Who cares if they can't buy today – they're a lead!

Stuff them in your pipeline, pitch your wares to anybody who will listen, and quickly you'll become a well-qualified shitty salesperson.

PUKE

Shitty Nick knew the value of puking. Nothing brought more attention to him than when he had the floor and puked all the information over the customer – forcing him to make a decision.

Just let it all out, *Exorcist*-style. Puking is the easiest sales lesson of all time. If you want to be a shitty salesperson, puke all the time and over everyone. What's puking? Talking. Talking about how awesome you are. Talk about all the features and benefits of your product. Talk about your terrible competition. Talk about sports, your kids, and the weather! Talk about how bad the competition is. Talk about how the market isn't changing. Talk about how terrible your boss is. Spend your time talking. Throw your notepad away, don't bother recording, don't ask any questions. In a word: Puke.

A key feature of puking is that you never allow the customer to ask a question. Tell them "hold on a second, I'll get there." or "wait one minute, I'm coming to that." As a *puke-er*, you don't explore, challenge, or assess their position. You walk into a meeting or start a webinar without building rapport. Then demonstrate your lack of homework and preparation and take the bull by the horns. The customer's job is to listen to you; your job is to tell them what's best for them.

Why puke? The only reason for puking is to get to the price. Price is the only thing that matters to shitty salespeople (and customers). The savviest buyers only buy on price. The faster you can get to the price, the better off. If you have the chance, start with price. Throw the price right out there, that way there's no hiding from it.

"This is what it costs Mr. Customer and here's all the great stuff that you're going to get. Sign here. Today. It's the best deal. You don't want to miss out."

A truism in life is to be memorable and what better way to be memorable than by puking on someone? That's your ticket to your title as a shitty salesperson.

DON'T DEVELOP EMOTINOAL INTELLIGENCE

Shitty Nick never bought the argument for emotional intelligence. Isn't it a made-up term used by snowflakes? Instead, he (and you should too), recognize that as a sales person, you deal with shit all the time. It's your right to blow it out of proportion. You want to have the same reaction to a lost sale, as you would to the unexpected death of your spouse.

You want to completely lose perspective and make sure that everybody knows and feels your misery, pain, and suffering. You want to continue to waste time, play the Woe-Is-Me card (super powerful), and outline various excuses as to what happened and how bad it is. Above all, you want to avoid thinking about how you can quickly repair and restore.

Strategies to remaining emotionally ignorant:

A. **Don't admit what happened**
   -No matter who is at-fault, don't find out the details. Make the customer bring the details to you. Have them do the investigation. If they won't go through that step, it's probably not a big deal.
   -Don't take the blame. The moment you take blame, you're on the hook for cleaning it up.
   -If the mess is a big one, treat it like a small one and if it's a small one, treat it like a big one. Over or underreacting will infuriate people and make the mess something it's not
B. **Don't put yourself in the customer's shoes**
   -Ignore the customer's perspective. Their perspective is wrong
   -Never Share the mess with the larger community. Keep things under wraps. Don't use this as a reason to do more work (be proactive). Let sleeping dogs lie
C. **Waste an "Awesome**!" experience
   -Tell the customer you'll have someone take care of the problem
   -If the solution is complex, don't give updates. Keep

them in the dark for as long as possible and until someone cleans up the mess
-Don't offer any restitution in money or services

These strategies merge with two other chapters: Never Have a Plan B and Always Have a Plan B. The ability to overreact is the perfect reason for not having a balance between *never* and *always*. Flying by the seat of your pants is the best way to go if you want an unexpected crash.
One of the joys of getting punched and not getting up is that you're probably not going to get punched again. A win! It's also easier to get kicked in the ass when you're laying down, but that's exactly what a shitty salesperson would want to have happened.

Here are 10 tactics to keep your emotional intelligence stunted

- Yell instead of speaking calmly
- Stay "down" instead getting "up."
- Show indifference at the serious
- Be grave about the insignificant
- Focus on excuses, not fixes
- Don't ask for a second opinion
- Make a call/Email when a face-to-face is better
- Go too high up the chain of command
- Don't breathe OR sleep on it
- Send defensive responses… immediately

The inability to balance proper response to stressful situations is a bona-fide qualification of a shitty salesperson. Don't hold back!

TRY NOTHING NEW

Shitty Nick knew what worked and what didn't. The more he tried something new, the more he failed. Finding one thing that worked is better than trying a hundred things that don't work.

If you've got a lead from phone calls, make more phone calls! Why take time away from things that work - to try something that may or may not work? Seems crazy to me. What if you try something new on a big prospect and it doesn't work? You risk losing the prospect. Plus aren't all prospects expecting the same process from every salesperson they talk to? Different is bad.

The process is simple: Say hi, talk about sports, then dive into your features and benefits. Next, list the price and tell the prospect to press hard because there are three copies. Tried and true.

Trying something new might get you in trouble with management, offend a customer, be an inconvenience... it might give an even better idea to your competitor. That would be the worst. If you're going to bother putting in the effort of trying something new, you must think hard about it. Who has time to think of something better? Then you've got to spend a lot of time working on a plan that may or may not work. What if it doesn't work? Now where's your position of strength? You might be expected to apologize for trying something that didn't work. Salespeople should never apologize.

A cardinal rule of being a shitty salesperson is never apologizing for anything at any time or for any reason. Experimentation is all about making thought-out, well-calculated risks. If you're busy making thought-out, well-calculated risks, how can you pick up the phone and make a cold call? You're too busy doing other stuff – like apologizing!

It's been said before and said again: none of your job descriptions ever talked about trying new things, developing new processes, or figuring out new ways to engage a customer. Hunt or farm, take your territory, call list, and go!

The phone works, email works, networking works. What more do you need? That much is enough if you want to be a shitty salesperson.

NEVER HAVE "PLAN B"

Shitty Nick rarely had "Plan B." Said another way, he never had an "oh shit!" button. But that's OK, because you, as an aspiring shitty sales person, want to have all your eggs in one basket. Always commit 100%. Give your company everything you can, all the time. Trust me; they'll return this loyalty ten-fold from your first day to right before you get fired.

You can't afford to ask: "what if things don't work out as planned?" You never want to consider what happens if the industry changes. You can't control it anyway, so what's the point? Never worry about how the sales process will change when decision makers change. Don't plan for disruptive technologies that will impact your pipeline. You have no control over these events, so wait for them to happen and react.

Don't bother asking yourself what you would do if you lost your biggest three customers. You'll easily find new ones. Don't consider what would happen if you lost your support staff; you'll find a new set of grunts. Don't worry about what happens when you go from a good sales manager to a bad manager – they're all out to hurt you anyway.

Having an "Oh shit!" button is terrible – what if your manager hears about it? How will they feel if you're moonlighting to follow your dream and not theirs? What does that say about your blind loyalty to the company and someone else's bonus?

And how are you supposed to develop Plan B? Get to know your customers and probable purchasers? Build strong relationships with people on your customer's team? That would mean going above and beyond their expectations and the time your company is willing to give to you. It would mean trying to be memorable in a world that only cares about price. Are you supposed to develop healthy relationships with your competition? It's not like they'd ever try to recruit you – never did to me!

Meet each day with open arms and whatever happens, happens. "What else is out there? What more can you do? How can you position yourself always to have an opportunity?" Those are dangerous questions, and they distract you from making your required cold calls. Give everything you can today to The Man. Tie all your success to his mercy. You can't afford to look to the horizon; focus on the here and now.

No, plan B? No problem! You're on your way to being shitty.

STOP LEARNING

Shitty Nick stopped learning because he had to start closing. Throughout his sales career, Shitty Nick got a job, learned the features and benefits, and hit the ground running. Your manager wants action – act! You don't have time to learn, experiment, and grow. Are you going to look at your manager at the end of the year, when you've hit 60% of your quota and say: "Hey boss, I know I was 40%, but I'm so much better at negotiating than I was when I started – can you up my commission to 8%?"

Once you know your features, benefits, and value proposition for your product or service, call, meet, follow-up, close, hand-ff to the Account Management team. Easy.

Someone might say that it's important to know why other people succeeded or failed. Respond: What would learning about the past success or failures of other people teach me? Obviously, I'm better than they are, that's why I'm here! Some people say it's good to go and learn why other people said "no." How would that help you? The problem was the previous person's inability to close.

Would learning about prior market dynamics help you today? How would predicting changes in your industry in three or five years help you today? Know what you need to know for today. You can't worry about the future. You can't think about why it would benefit you to increase your skill set. What if you invest in one area and you come to find out that it's not applicable? You just wasted all that time. You certainly weren't closing while you were learning!

And really, as if learning how to learn is a skill you can develop! You went to school; you passed your classes, you got your job, you went through training; learning is done. You wouldn't be in sales if you didn't already know it all. You're in the trenches. Just like Blain Cooper "didn't have time to bleed" you don't have time to learn. Quota. Closing. Money. That's what matters.

Today, you're all about doing. If something changes in your industry, relax and watch *The Kardashian's,* then watch a YouTube video on it. Simple problem, simple solution. Is learning cold calling, negotiating, and closing? You're already an expert! What are the odds of taking a class helping you close more business today? Zero.

On the off-chance that continuing education is a requirement, isn't it always just the same stuff repackaged year after year? You pay your $35 for the three-hour class, get the credits, and move on. Those classes are ways for other people to *make money off of you*. Your goal as a salesperson is to *make money off of other people*. *Learning* steals from *closing*.

I got my MBA, $75,000; didn't learn a thing. Look how I turned out. I still don't know how to sell, plus do the teachers know what you're going through? Is the curriculum even that applicable? If the teacher was in the industry for decades, and now is teaching, isn't it possible they can no longer cut it in the industry, and so that's why they went to teaching it? What could you possibly learn from those dinosaurs? They're extinct for a reason.

Don't bother learning anything new. Pick up the phone, get the meeting, sign the papers, get your check. That's what a shitty salesperson needs to learn.

DON'T HELP OTHER SALESPEOPLE SELL

Shitty Nick never helped other salespeople sell because he knew that if he helped them, he was ultimately hurting himself. Do you ever see an alligator help another alligator kill a wildebeest? It's survival of the fittest and in order to be the fittest, you've got to be the shittiest.

If you've made it this far in the book and haven't picked up on a theme, here it is: if the activity you are doing does not help you meet your quota, don't do it. "Helping someone sell" sits square in the middle of "behaviors to avoid." How can you benefit from helping someone else out with their business development problem? Helping other people sell is fraught with many perils; but it's veiled in the grotesque mask of "nice, friendly, helpful, and being a team player." You know what? How does being nice, friendly, helpful, and a team player help you close your own business?

If a coworker comes to you with a sales problem, your answer should be, "Mr. Salesperson, that's your problem. Go figure it out." That honest, straightforward advice forces them to grow as a salesperson and not rely on other people as a crutch. By not helping them, you're helping them. Everybody wins. Think about it this way: if you are helping someone else, are you prospecting? Are you negotiating? Are you closing? Are you servicing your accounts? No, you're helping somebody else do the stuff that they should be doing by themselves.

Obviously, you've never had to ask for help. You have figured out the sales process, how to work with customers, solve problems, and meet challenges by yourself. Think of what could happen if you help someone else. First, your manager is going to see that you're not doing what he's paid you to do. Enjoy that conversation in your annual review. Second, when you help a fellow salesperson, you help them be potentially better than you. What's next? They steal your business. Lose, lose, and lose.

Nice guys finish last. Just go back and look at your job description. Does it say anywhere how you should be a team player, help other people grow and develop, and expand your horizons through teamwork? How is collaboration a requirement of your job? It's not, so why do it?

Be the lone ranger, force people to figure things out on their own (nobody's ever helped you), and you're likely to earn a title worthy of your business card: Shitty Salesperson.

CONCEDE EVERYTHING

Shitty Nick excelled at giving away the farm because he knew that whatever he had to do to get the sale, whether it is price, terms, implementation... whatever the customer asked, he'd say: "Yes!"

It is not your responsibility to worry about whether the customer is easy to service customer or even profitable. How the new customer helps the long-term forecast of your company's business is not your concern. As a salesperson you have one goal: get people to buy, so you get paid.

Shouldn't management worry about margins, terms, and profitability? Once you get people to say "yes" and you've got your commission check, stop caring. Business is better than no business, right? If the customer is comfortable with the terms and price, get them to sign it! Bring a signed contract to your manager and let your manager turn that deal down.

You're the one who faces rejection every day. Let your manager face that awkward position of taking the business that they don't like or not agreeing to what you've done. Now it's your manager's problem. The more blindly you serve your customer, the less likely you are to face uncomfortable situations like rejection.

You want two things, to get paid and to make your customer feel good (the latter is a bonus). You're not responsible for the long-term strategic goals of the organization. That's above your pay and responsibility grade. Who cares if the business you write is bad business? Who cares if it doesn't make the company a lot of money? Who cares if that customer is a pain in the ass to the account management or customer service team? Not your problem. Let your company worry about the time and resources customers use up. You've got other fish to fry.

Salespeople get paid for one thing: prospects signing on the dotted line. If you're not focused on that, you're wasting energy. And if not you, then who? Encourage customers to put down as little money upfront. Give the legal team as little as possible to work with – they kill business anyway. Help prospects say "Yes!" Why should customers have skin in the game? Try to wave management's stupid terms they put in to "protect the company." If you're safe, that's all that matters.

Isn't it a great feeling bringing a signed contract to your sales manager that they couldn't reject because they're worried about their bonus? They'll handle problems if their bonus rides on it.

Do whatever is necessary to have the customer sign on the dotted line. The ensuing commission (and management's pain and suffering) will concede a simple point: you're a shitty salesperson.

SANDBAG

Shitty Nick was an expert sandbagger. It's one of the best shitty sales tricks! As a salesperson, remember that you are always under the microscope of your manager and that they are always looking for a reason to fire you or a reason to lower your commission schedule. What's the best way to avoid that? Never be in the top 10% or bottom 15-20%. How do you do that? Sandbag.

If you're in the top 10%, you might get some accolades like President's Club or be asked to give your opinion or invited to work on a complicated issue. What will that do? You guessed it, take time away from your cold calling and negatively impact your numbers. People will see you as a leader, there will be added pressure, and if you fail, your job (and paycheck) is on the line. Plus, if you're great, you might get poached by another company who's probably going to offer you more money and a bigger title, but then, you're forced to start all over because you signed a non-compete or some other binding document. Better to be a big fish in a small pond and play where you can't lose.

If you're in the bottom 20%, you're probably going to get fired, and that's the last thing you want. You want to try to be that no-name salesperson who comes to work, hits a reasonable number, and then goes home. You don't want to draw too much attention to yourself. If you want to avoid those two unenviable positions, you'll need to sandbag.

A bit confused on the sandbagging process? Don't worry – below is your step-by-step guide.

1) Set a daily quota of activity
    - once you make X calls, stop
    - once you make Y meetings, stop
    - once you make z sales, stop
    - following this process will ensure that you never get too much business at one time

2) Delay meetings
   - perhaps the greatest strategy, if you can push a meeting off a week and get it into the next week/month/quarter it can't be closed today!

3) Put up artificial barriers
   - if you know the customer is going to say "yes" create a delay in the date your business is counted as "closed."
   - tell customers about next quart'ers dicscount
   - tell them there's a technical difficulty
   - make a mistake with the order process

4) Turn in paperwork late / post-date
   - add a week onto delivery
   - tell them to post-date a contract/check

How good was Shitty Nick at sandbagging? Once he had a job where if he did X in a month, he got a $500 car allowance. Do you think he ever did any more than X+1? Nope! What if the customer had to wait? Big deal! Sandbagging is a great way to put your numbers right where YOU want them. Your numbers are *your* numbers. Who cares what your manager wants or your customer needs? It's not like customers pay your commission check – your company does!

Do it right, and you can sandbag your way to be the ultimate shitty salesperson.

PEDESTALIZE YOUR SALES MANAGER

Shitty Nick loved kissing ass because it showed his manager and coworkers that he was a great team player.

First, believe that your sales manager is the end-all-be-all salesperson. They think it's true. Just look at how good they are at prospecting and customer engagement. Admire how they handle complex negotiations. Be impressed with their ability to stay firm on price and not make concessions for their favorite salespeople.

First, believe that your sales manager is the end-all-be-all salesperson. They think it's true. Just look at how good they are at prospecting and customer engagement. Admire how they handle complex negotiations. Be impressed with their ability to stay firm on price and not make concessions for their favorite salespeople.

Second, be awed by their ability always to get their bonus. If YOU focus on this area alone, you'll never think of taking steps to get your sales manager fired when that might be the best move for you and your organization. Play it safe all the time.

Third, don't worry about the roadblocks that they put up. Don't wonder why they always seem to be covering their ass first. Whatever you do, never muster the courage to tell your boss's boss what you think of your boss. Your senior managers aren't interested in your critical thoughts. They're not interested in your ability to take a stand. They don't want to see you put your neck out on the line and they certainly don't want to see you selling them on an idea on how to make the business better. They want you selling their product. It's not your job to demonstrate critical thinking skills. It's your job to sell.

Finally, don't highlight your manager's inefficiencies. Don't try to figure out what customers need or to demonstrate how the current sales process (implemented by your manager) is working against everyone's best interests. Leave all of that to your sales manager. They're your manager for a reason, and it's because they're a lot smarter than you, more experienced, and understand the business better than you.

Sit back, relax, be pushed around at the whims of your direct manager and you will be atop the pedestal of shitty salespersons.

ONLY RESPOND TO RFPs

Shitty Nick knew that the best route to getting on a prospect's good side was to wait for the RFP. He understood that if he was involved early-on in the process, then that time and energy would take away from closing. Better to wait to be told what to do than to take any initiative.

You've got to understand that as a salesperson your job is to show the customer what you have, how it solves their problem, and the cost. That's how sales works. Why in the world would you want to get involved in helping the customer draft up the RFP? What if that opened the door for exposure to you not having exactly what they need? What if in that process it revealed that maybe your product was too expensive, too hard to implement, or too difficult to compare to other standard options?

Relax and wait for the prospect to define the solution. Your job is to get the peg in the hole – who cares what shape it is? What could you gain by helping them define the requirements? Nothing but more work. When you respond to the RFP, you can couch things so that they make you look to be the best. Besides, it's not like your competition would actively work with the customer to understand the problem and then customize a solution that fits their offerings perfectly – you and your competition share the same fears!

What if your product can't do what your prospect needs? How could you benefit from being involved in the process when you know you're already behind the eight ball? What if you go through that process and during that process, the customer finds out that they need something that's going to take away from your sales dollars? What good have you done? You'll help them spend money (elsewhere), but it won't help your commission check this quarter.

When you get involved in the RFP process, you will sap time, energy, and resources from the product, engineering, and marketing teams... maybe even from management. If you get all these other people involved, you'll have to manage them. They could screw it up by saying something wrong because they're not sales experts – they don't have your skill set. It's a nightmare! And then when the customer says "no" who does management blame? You!

You want to wait for the RFP to arrive in your inbox. Then fill in the blanks. That's how you show how your product is perfect for what they've requested. Helping customers draft RFPs requires work, creativity, and determination. Go ahead, do all that, but remember, it all comes down to price.

If you've done your job by dotting all their "I's" and crossing all their "T's," you'll have done the same for becoming a sh**itt**y salesperson.

BUILD YOUR EXCUSE MACHINE

Shitty Nick had the *Rube Goldberg* ***Excuse Machine.*** Through an intricate series of pullies, levers, and ramps, he built a machine that gave him an excuse for every bad situation. Want your own Excuse Machine?Lucky you! Here are the components and instructions!

1. The customer is not ready for your solution
2. The customer is going through internal change and can't make purchase decisions
3. The customer just bought from the competition
4. The customer wouldn't take your phone call or meeting
5. The customer has internal politics you can't overcome
6. The customer said, "The product was too expensive"
7. The customer said, "Our service isn't good enough"
8. The customer said, "Our solution is too old"
9. The customer said, "They are changing business lines and don't need us
10. The customer said that they needed more time
11. The customer said, "come back in a year"
12. The customer lied about being the real decision maker
13. The customer is related to the competition
14. The customer says they have a master agreement with the competition

The reason customers don't buy and the responsibility for customers not buying is always the customer's fault. It is never your fault. Obviously, you have the best product, service, and pricing. You know how to engage and influence. But let's be honest, customers are dumb. Customers make mistakes all the time. It's obvious that when they say "no" to you, they are making a mistake and it's no reflection on your abilities.

To ensure that you have a job next month, you need to be able to pinpoint the reasons for the customer not buying from you. As you can see from the list, you must always shape the rejection as the mistake the customer made and demonstrated how none of it was your fault. You can't be fired if it wasn't your fault, right?

Use these parts to build your Excuse Machine, and you'll have no excuse for not becoming a shitty salesperson.

ALWAYS REACT

Shitty Nick mastered reaction. He knew there was no point in preparing for unexpected inconveniences or major disruptions because there's no point in trying to predict the future. There is no point in trying to figure out how to be at the right place at the right time. It's like trying to time the market; nobody can do it.

How do you master becoming a reactive salesperson? The first (and most important thing you do is **never** make the first call. Wait for the customer's call or email to come to you.

Once they've shared everything, tell them you will get back to them with an idea or two. You don't want to throw out a possible solution right away because if you do, and you're right, they will expect that kind of behavior. What if you make a mistake? Can you risk a mistake? No way, you've got a quota to make. Which leads to Point #2: wait for customers to bring a known problem to your attention. Here's how that works:

Don't ever call customers about a possible problem. This is similar to the previous idea but what you're doing in this step is ensuring you don't create an issue when one doesn't exist. Let sleeping dogs lie. If they say, "I wish you would've called me beforehand" you can say something like "I didn't expect this to happen. We haven't heard about this issue before. Nobody else has had this problem. We wanted to make sure that we had a viable solution before we brought anything to your attention." That type of approach shows that you're trying to care and think through things even though you couldn't care less (especially if you've already cashed your commission check).

For example, if your company has a data breach, why would you want to tell everybody that you had a data breach? Only reach out to the customers who you absolutely know had an issue and then wait until later (or never) to tell the rest? This way, you can focus your resources only on the people that you know have had an issue, and then wait to see what happens after that. Call it the

Equifax Approach, or the Target Approach, or the Home Depot Approach. Customers forget about this stuff, so why push it any further than necessary?

Wait and see what happens after an issue pops up. Try to gauge the (possible) level of anger and disappointment in your customer. Don't engage them before you need to, and you'll give them the perfect way to react to you being a shitty salesperson.

THE POWER OF 9:00 AM TO 5:00 PM

Shitty Nick knew, just like being anti-social was critical to his mental health, that 9-5 is where the money was at. To help you see that these are the best hours to interact with decision-makers, you need to destroy a few myths.

The first myth is that owners and decision-makers are always in the office early, so you need to be in the office early to reach them. That's ridiculous. If a decision maker is in the office early, shouldn't you be courteous of her time? Maybe this is her only chance to get important work done. Who are you to interrupt it?

That begs the question, how early is early enough? Does it need to be 8:00, 7:30, 7:00, 6:30? If this were such a wise idea, you would need to be prepared to give a potential customer a call at almost any hour of the day. Ridiculous! How are you supposed to know what their schedule is? Are you going to have their direct dial? If that decision-maker gets an early morning call, they're of course going to expect that it's something urgent and important that could change their business, so if that's not you (and it rarely is), wait until after 9 AM.

The second myth is that lunchtime is a great time to call. How are you going to refuel if you're calling? And don't decision makers eat lunch? Would you like it if someone cold called you during your lunch? Don't even think about "dropping in" at lunch – the gatekeeper might not be there - how can you gain access if someone can't let you in? Decision makers have a lot on their plate... Interrupting personal lunchtime will makes prospects mad, and you don't want to make them mad. Shitty salespeople never make decision makers feel uncomfortable.

The last myth is that owners stay late and are willing to take calls after 5:00 PM. Don't believe it! Owners come in and out as they please and never stay late. Instead of waiting around to make after-hours calls, prepare for tomorrow's calls, and tomorrow's sales meetings, and tomorrow's closes. And today's happy hour!

As a salesperson, you're not paid for your time; you're paid for your output, so only put out and perform during those optimal business hours of 9:00 AM to 5:00 PM. That's the perfect time to become a shitty salesperson.

10 STEPS TO AVOID REJECTION

Shitty Nick avoided rejection at every opportunity. You're not paid to be rejected, you're paid to be accepted! Rejection is for losers. Rejection is for masochists. Here's the *how* and *why* to avoiding rejection.

Use email instead of cold calls to find new business
    Email rejection is easier than face-to-face any day
Only make the minimum number of calls/emails per day
    If your number is 20, do 20 – fewer rejections
Never ask for a referral
    referrals are dangerous to give and perilous to act on, stay away
Only use social media to connect with buyers
    Without likes/follows/retweets, you get rejected, but no pain!
Always give the buyer an easy way out
    "How about I circle-back in a year?"
Don't follow up (and never follow through
    Cut off communication and **you** do the rejecting
Never build a relationship with the final decision maker
    They're too important, stick with the "users."
Remain ignorant of the buying process
    Ignorance of rejection is bliss!
Only go for easy sales
    Without a choice, they can't reject you
Never ask for the sale
    If you don't ask, they can't say no!

Rejection doesn't have to be *your* reality. Follow these steps and painlessly become a shitty salesperson.

NEVER APOLOGIZE

Shitty Nick never apologized because it was never his fault. Customers understand that the salesperson can't be blamed for their experience. Something went wonky in the process. If you step-up and try to take some (or God-forbid, ALL) of the blame, people will view you in a totally new light. Is that what you want?

Never apologize for any reason. It is not your fault. That's the truth. The prospect decided to be a customer. The prospect decided to implement. Problems now fall to the Customer Support and Service teams. The contract was clear (enough). You gave the prospect a full product description. If something goes wrong, it's not your fault because if it's your fault, then you've got to take ownership, then you need to make a point on fixing it, then you must bear the humiliation.

What next? You get to deal with all the brain damage from your boss. You get to deal with the customer service team. You get to engage with the marketing team. You get to tell the Product Team. And on and on and on! But, if you are wise enough never to apologize, you can deflect until the very end of your career and never have to own anything that went wrong. Why should you apologize for a product not working right? Why should you apologize for implementation not happening as smooth as the customer expected? You're paid to sell it, that's it.

Where did customers get that idea that implementation would be easy? Why did they think service would be great? You'd never make any promises like that. It's not your fault you said anything you needed to say to get the sale. Isn't having a problem like this much better than *not* having a sale? Everyone knows that you are empowered and obligated to say anything and everything you need to for the customer to sign on the dotted line. Because you are empowered and obligated there should be no reason that you ever feel the need to take one on the chin for something not going perfectly.

Let the other business units apologize. Let them explain what's going on. Let them fix the problem. Do they ever apologize if you don't get contracts? Didn't think so. If you're busy apologizing, explaining, and fixing, then you're not closing. See, you are the relationship guy. How in the world can you help your relationship if you're walking up to them with your tail between their legs because something wasn't perfect?

In the commercial world, buyers must beware. Now, maybe you have a fiduciary duty to your customer, so don't break the law... but... isn't it reasonable to think that you're doing what you need to do to stay in business, so you get paid, so that you can help them buy again next year? See that? Doesn't it seem like you staying in business is good for them? Why should anyone complain? And why should you apologize? Follow this axiom: it's the buyer's job to beware, but it's not your job to help them be aware.

If you can shift blame and to take attention away from you, you'll never have to apologize for being a shitty salesperson.

SKIP HUMOR

Shitty Nick was never funny. Customers don't want to laugh, they want to be sold. Don't try to be funny – stick to features, benefits, and price.

Humor is tough. Some people are just naturally funny and if you work on being funny, how is that working on being a good salesperson? If you are a funny guy, then you're setting yourself up for disaster, because as soon as you start making people laugh, they will listen to you. They will expect something funny and for you to tie humor to their critical business issue.

It's one thing to tell a joke; it's another thing to throw out a few quick quips and deliver your message in a light but powerful way. Aren't you better off being straightforward and to the point? Prospects don't want you to be funny. They don't need you to be funny. They need you to give them a solution to their problem as cheap as possible.

The other problem with humor is that you must be careful with it. You can't go around telling inappropriate jokes (no matter how funny), so if you can't tell the best joke, why bother telling any joke? To be funny you need to spend a lot of time understanding your audience, their personal and cultural background, and how your joke might land with them.

You can't do comedy willy-nilly, you're going to have to learn. You might have to spend some time watching comedy. You might be forced to go and try and do stand-up on your own. What good it would do you to stand up on stage and to face an audience? How could that possibly help you in the board room, in the heat of the moment when it's time to ask for the deal?

Be formal, be polished, play it tight. Again, if you're funny, prospects will to listen to you and pay attention to you. That leaves you no room to sneak by a dramatic increase of price, tightened terms, or problems. If they're paying attention to every word, you have to say because you're funny, they'll hear everything else. That doesn't sound very funny.

Being shitty is no laughing matter and never the mark of a shitty salesperson.

DON'T COME WITH IDEAS

Shitty Nick was not an "idea guy." Ideas are a dime-a-dozen. Customers want solutions, cheap. If you give ideas, you give yourself more work.

If you can make your mantra as a person who is "Idea-*less*" you won't be forced to do the hard work necessary to make sales easy. It also helps you set the bar low, and it gives you the freedom to fly by the seat of your pants to show yourself as a free-wheeling, on-the-fly guy who can handle any situation – true or not!

To provide ideas to your prospect about how they win with you, you need a creative brain (especially if you're new and you don't have a lot of experience). If you come in guns-blazing with ideas, then your customer will expect fantastic results from you. Why would you want to set the bar that high? Why would you want to set yourself up for failure? The first thing you want to do is read the chapter about not doing homework. Because the sooner you do homework, the sooner you've got ideas. And ideas are dangerous and powerful – but not as powerful as price!

Once you have ideas, you've got to set high expectations. Once you set high expectations, you need to deliver. Big mistake! Go to a sales meeting without any ideas. Play the role of the blank slate; the sponge that's there to listen and hear the customer complain. The prospect will tell you everything. Prospects happily open-up about pain points, lack of efficiencies, limited profitability, and about the politics that go into this decision. Happens all the time, right? Just listen and skip note-taking.

If you come to the table with lots of ideas, your customer might ask you about things not directly related to the sales presentation you're there to deliver. Hear it again: if it doesn't directly help you close the business, don't worry about it. It's of no value to you. You're not their psychologist; you're their salesperson. Ideas are the first step to over-promising and over-delivering –

a dangerous gamble! You want to under-promise because takes very little effort to over-deliver. It's brilliant.

Ideas are powerful, require action, and they're hard to kill. If you give the wrong idea to your customer, then you've set yourself up for massive failure. It's simply not worth the risk. Do your sales meeting but don't come with ideas. Don't come with solutions. Don't come with answers. Don't come with new information that could help them. What could you possibly know before you talk to them anyway?

Follow that route, and you'll have a great idea on how to be a shitty salesperson.

USE CLICHES

Shitty Nick mastered clichés. It's a no-brainer activity that will empower you to increase your bandwidth and give you the most bang for your buck. Customers will see that you speak their language and together, you'll make a lot of hay.

What's a cliché? Think of how an athlete or a coach talks in a post-game interview. It's all clichés.

A lot of salespeople are athletes, so hopefully, this advice hits home and really sticks. Clichés and a lack of details are the hallmarks of coaches and athletes during a post-game interview. Talk to customers about squaring the circle, happy but not satisfied, synergies, moving the goalposts, and win-win; especially win-win. See, it's easy!

Win-win makes the customer believe you want them to win more than you. Try to get the ball rolling by biting the bullet and ensuring that customers compare apples to apples. When pressed on the nuts and bolts of the problem, reply with moving targets. For example, when a customer asks how a critical component of implementation will take place, tell them that you are taking care of all the blocking and tackling so they can focus on pushing the ball downfield.

Using clichés, especially tired and overused clichés, helps you avoid concrete answers. Just speak with an air of authority. Tell prospects you will focus on fundamentals so they can focus on their game plan. If something goes wrong, tell them you are increasing bandwidth to address future hurdles. If they ask you how you will accomplish a difficult task, tell them you'd love to share, but you can't open the kimono.

You want to offer the most indirect responses you can without the prospect completely losing faith in you. You want them to think that they may not understand what you've said because you weren't specific but because you said it in such a confident voice and with a relatable topic that you must have the situation under control. A little exaggeration might also go a long way in making them believe you know what you're talking about. Done right, by the time they realize the mistake they made with you, they are in too deep, can't put on the brakes, and you'll get paid.

Have faith! Anyone, even you, can square that circle and become a shitty salesperson.

IGNORE BUYING SIGNALS

Shitty Nick always ignored buying signals because he had a message and vision to share – the prospect needed to listen to him!

Fact: customers are not good poker players and will reveal when they are interested in buying. If you ignore those signals, you are going to blow right by all the opportunities for them to say "yes!" What are the buying signals you should ignore?

The first buying signal is a question about you. If they are interested in you and use their time talking about you, this is a clear signal that they want to buy. Change the subject, fast!

Next are detailed questions about your product or service perform, and how they relate to the prospect's specific situation. Holy crap, this means they are interested in what you have to offer. Respond vaguely. Don't make any promises and certainly don't speak with an air of authority or confidence.

The third signal is a question about the implementation process. If they're at this stage, they're 90% of the way to buying. This is where *seeds of doubt* perform best. Focus on challenges the customer may encounter. Talk about a few problems that exist with your product or service. Complain about management or highlight the benefits of a competitor.

Fourth, once you get a verbal commitment. How do you do that? Be unresponsive. Don't show any interest or excitement. Absolutely avoid trying to increase the size of the sale at this point by offering ancillary products and services.

Finally, be indifferent about what they want to accomplish and the success they'll get by using your product. Don't thank them for business. Don't offer an "implementation plan." Just ask when you can expect the contract and check.

If you can ignore these buying signals, you'll send up the signal that you're a shitty salesperson.

DON'T WORRY ABOUT BEING LIKED

Shitty Nick knew that "being liked" was an excuse used by sales people who struggled learning features and benefits. Customers don't like you, won't like you, and can't like you – unless you offer the cheapest price.

Jeffrey Gitomer says that all things being equal, people prefer to do business with people that they like, and all things being not so equal, people still prefer to do business with people that they like. Maybe, but most things aren't equal, and most customers only purchase on price, so what's the point in being liked?

Wouldn't you rather be respected for who you are, and that is a person who's a straight-shooter on price? Being liked means you might have to change how you operate. Shouldn't to your self be true? Being liked might mean you have to change your attitude, but your attitude makes you who you are; it's how you got here in the first place.

Point-of-order: what is likable? It's a moving target for everybody. Maybe it means you are kind and thoughtful. Maybe it means you're funny and easygoing. Maybe it means you give a lot of value first. Or maybe it just means you're different from the last sales guy and the customer doesn't care at all about you, they're just trying to do something new.

Do you see how tough it is to be likable? How can you possibly be all these things? Since customers buy on price, what is like worth? I'm pretty sure that you are like me and only give your money to the person with the best price. Why would your customer be any different?

Do you think being likable could be enough to get you past the gatekeeper? Do you think being likable could give you a second chance? Could being likable help, you make a new connection? Maybe, but it's nowhere near as powerful as saying, "I've got the best price for this widget!" When's the last time a customer told you that you lost their business because they liked somebody more than you? Probably never. You probably only lose on price, so focus on price, be liked because of price; don't make them tolerate your price because they like you.

Try this one out for size: as you're filling out your CRM for your boss, is there a column that highlights how much the prospect likes you and you can use that "like" to get the sale? Didn't think so. You're better off focusing on cold calls and price than you are trying to build any semblance of a relationship with somebody who's just going to drop you as soon as a better price comes along.

Sure, it may be easier to be respected if people like you, but it's a lot easier to be a shitty salesperson when you're not.

MAKE IT HARD TO SAY "YES!"

Shitty Nick knew the value in making it difficult for the customer to say "Yes!" Do you think if you can make it easy, you'll own the experience? When has a prospect picked a better experience over price. The craziest thing Shitty Nick ever heard was: "if you own the experience, you own the customer." No, if you own the price, you own the customer.

If you want to slow things down, put up roadblocks to "Yes!" If the process of getting to "Yes" is difficult, there's no way that they're going to buy, which means that there is far less work for you to do: fewer meetings, fewer calls, fewer accounts to manage - less of everything. So how do you throw a wrench in the sales gears?

1) Make lots of forms. Paperwork = Frustrations = slower sales
2) Always get the legal team involved. Customers love going through redlines your legal team could have easily removed but chose not to because they believe it's better to CYA than to make money
3) Have customers go to multiple places/business units before the deal is official. This helps you make other groups feel important and put up the guise of a deeply thought-out process when it's all unnecessary.
4) Make-up "contract review dates." Customers love hearing that they must wait to implement because of your company's internal process.
5) Don't have an escape clause. Customers like the security of knowing they can't ever turn back, that there is no refund policy, and that they have a disproportionate amount of skin in the game.

What do these things have in common? For most purchases, they're completely unnecessary. Sure, lots of work and parameters need to happen for "enterprise" level purchases, but that doesn't mean that level of detail can't exist in a more transactional environment.

Making it difficult to say "yes!" helps you sandbag. You know how sales operations and implementation work at your company, the customer doesn't! Use their lack of knowledge to your benefit.

Treat customers like a puppet, you've got the strings, and the show is you performing as a shitty salesperson.

PUT YOUR CUSTOMER'S NEEDS LAST

Shitty Nick made sure that his needs were the priority because only if Nick got paid could everyone win. The correct "hierarchy of sales needs" is: salesperson, company, then customer.

The best way to ignore the needs of your customer is to maximize your commission. If you're worried about your commission, then you will abuse resources, energies, and attitudes by pulling them away from your customer. If you're worried about how a deal will impact your bottom line, you will pay less attention to the bottom line of your customer and your company.

People will argue that you should meet the customer's needs first, but if you disregard the customer's needs, it's a lot easier to meet the needs of you and your company. That's what a boss wants to see. This is a great way that you can show loyalty to yourself and to your company. Your company signs your check, shouldn't you respond with primary loyalty?

Your company also has needs for you to meet. If the customer is a PITA, while not your primary concern, do you want to create bad blood between you and the account management team? No! The relationship with your coworkers is more important than the relationship with your customer. The way to handle this is to charge the customer more. If your company gets more money, they'll tolerate more shit. Isn't your company the entity that hires and fires you? Where should your loyalties lie? Remember office space and the big question "Is this good for the company?" That's what you should ask yourself.

Is the prospect's solution also good for your boss? Is the sale good for your team? If the answer to that is always yes, then you are doing a great job of flipping the hierarchy of sales needs upside down. That's exactly what a shitty salesperson does. Focus on the short term, on today, on profitability, on making sure the customer does one thing, and that is: press hard when they sign because there are three copies.

If you put the needs of the customer first, then by default you're taking away from yourself and your company. Isn't making the company money so they can pay you money the primary goal? Isn't the customer just a means to an end for you?

The biggest secret to this activity is sharing your commission breath. If the prospect can smell your desire for the sale, they'll know exactly how much you value them and their success. Don't be shy about it and don't try to hide it with *Sales Listerine* (the tempering of your win in the transaction done by doing more than you're paid to do).

Shitty salespeople understand the best way to put the sales puzzle together is first you, then company, followed by the customer. Simple!

FORGET TRAINING AND DEVELOPMENT

Shitty Nick worked hard to avoid every training opportunity because he knew that if he wanted to hit quota, training and development killed closing time.

The bigger problem with training? Is it ever applicable? Think about it: you get all these people who may have or maybe haven't sold a lot of stuff in life trying to tell you what you need to do to sell. As if their history applies to what you need to do and your situation – the nerve! Have they made **your** cold calls? Have they done **your** meetings? Have they dealt with **your** sales manager? Have they been in **your** trenches?

No way. What could these "experts" have to say that would benefit you? Most of their books and classes are only a way to prey on your desire to make more money. Are they interested in making you a better salesperson or is the real motivation book sales? Do you think they have your best interests in mind?

What if you go to a class on "professional development?" You know you'll have to roleplay - like that's really what happens on a sales call or in a meeting! Maybe the trainer will try to challenge your beliefs and attitude, but who are they to challenge something that's inherently yours? Who's to say your beliefs and attitudes are wrong? That's arrogant.

You know who you are. You know what you believe. You know how you think. You know what customers want. You know how to make them listen. You know how to make them sign on the dotted line. What do these "trainers" know? They know how to stand up in front of a room and talk. They know how to write a book. They know how to make people laugh, feel, and think. That's not your job. You've got to sell. When you don't make your quota, whose fault is it? Your fault.

What if you do what the teacher tells you to do and you don't make quota? Is your boss going to fire the trainer? No way.

Hopefully, you've worked long enough to collect six months of unemployment. It can't emphasize it enough: your job description does not say that you should grow, develop, and mature as a salesperson.

Your compensation comes from selling; not training, developing, or growing. Follow that path and without even training you'll develop naturally into a shitty salesperson.

PRESENT, DON'T PERFORM

Shitty Nick knew that prospects want one thing when it comes to a meeting: a simple list of features, benefits, and price. Everything else is fluff that keeps you away from happy hour and them from...something. Think you've got what it takes to perform? Take a look at this list: you probably couldn't even act the part of a great salesperson.

1) Don't become the character. Watch any good actor, and you'll see that they're not just "acting," but *living* their character. The actor doesn't just know what the character says; the actor knows what the character thinks and believes. How do you do this? Don't think and believe like a great salesperson. You don't have to try and be terrible; you can settle with mediocrity. Show up, check the "sales activity" boxes, and you'll have checked the first box of "non-performance."
2) Don't know your audience. Don't even care that you don't know your audience. Your lack of emotional connection can have a 1:1 correlation with your level of shittiness. Don't worry about mutual connections. Don't become an expert in the industry they serve. Don't do the kind of homework that would put you in position to challenge their business assumption. Worrying about what makes them tick and what makes them happy is an exercise in futility. All customers are the same – they only care about price.
3) Don't be prepared. If you're unprepared, you can't engage, compel, cause the prospect to listen and create a buying environment. Don't have a checklist of everything you need to bring to a meeting. Always run out of business cards. Don't keep your LinkedIn profile up-to-date. Don't read "trade rags" or follow industry influencers. If you can price your product 10% less than the competition, you've got a fighting chance.
4) Don't take joy in your work. Look, it's a job. Nothing

more. Your company doesn't care about you; your customer doesn't care about you, so don't care about them. What sales job is enjoyable? They're all the same. Smile and dial for dollars. You've probably (or will) sell for ten companies in your life and believe each one was your ticket to happiness. It's not. There's nothing to enjoy.

5) Give up. When the going gets tough, the shitty salesperson gets going... to the easier sales job. Get rejected? Don't fight. Have a bad manager. Quit. Industry changing faster than you? Find a new one. What's the point in trying to grow and improve when everyone's out to make it tougher for you – from your support staff to your manager to your customer?

Some say that sales are the stage on which business is performed. Well, if that's true, follow these steps, and you'll win an Oscar for Shittiest Salesperson.

DON'T PROSPECT OUTSIDE OF THE OFFICE

Shitty Nick knew the best place to find a customer was by sitting in the office and making calls – lots and lots of calls. That's what prospects expect, that's what you should do.

You're probably thinking: how can you be a salesperson without prospecting in more than one way? Easy – torpedo all your external activities through laziness, willful ignorance, and rudeness.

How do you be lazy? Do every external activity without a plan, or if you do plan, make that plan be about you. Think networking: if you decide to go with a plan, make it a plan about you – not how you can help other people in the room – but how other people can help you. You shouldn't be there to help other people. Don't be known as a valuable resource, a connector, or someone that might create an experience for others. Don't stand out or take a chance. Certainly, don't be an official speaker. Forget your business cards and leave your phone in the car – those two things are great to avoid making connections.

Remain socially ignorant by avoiding social, community, and charity groups. These are places where decision-makers go because decision-makers are often movers and shakers in their community. If you're there, then you're going to have to be on-point. Is that why you're there? If you do go, start selling immediately. Don't worry about building a connection or a relationship. You've already found common ground; you're both in the same spot, you both care about the same thing, what more does the prospect need?

Finally, just be rude. You're a salesperson. You're a big deal. People should feel lucky to have you there and be exposed to everything you have to offer. When you answer a question, be terse. When you ask a question, look at the person offering a response in a bored or dismissive way. If you're asked to help at an event, make sure you get something in return – everything is a transaction.

In short, only rely on the phone and Email to do your prospecting, but if you must go outside your office, be lazy, ignorant, and rude. Sales is a numbers game, and calls and Emails are the only numbers you can put in your CRM. That's what your manager wants and that's how your graded.

If you follow the steps above when it comes to out-of-office prospecting, your prospects of becoming a shitty salesperson will go through the roof!

MANIPULATE

Shitty Nick wasn't much of magician, but he had one great trick: manipulation. It's easy to learn and use in every aspect of your life to get people to do what you want them to do.

Manipulation is not an easy skill to develop, but if you hone your manipulation skills, there is almost nothing you can't get. Let's answer the obvious: is manipulation all that bad? Isn't that what good salespeople do? Isn't that what persuasive people do all the time? They manipulate people's feelings, reactions, and thoughts to get them to go along with the salesperson's plans. If it's your plan, well, obviously, your plan and what you're doing and what you're offering are superior to what they're doing today or anything else that's out in the marketplace. In a word: no.

Why does manipulation get a bad rap? Aren't you helping people see things from a different perspective? Is it really that bad of a thing to force someone into a decision that may or may not benefit them? Here's your guide to prospect manipulation.

First, manipulate your customer's thoughts. You do that by twisting their thoughts inside out. Let's say the customer has a revenue problem. What you want to do then is focus on the ability for them to cut costs and not worry about making money. At the end of the day, isn't it all profit? Customer says, "We are trying to make more money." You say, "I can help you cut costs." See, that's the same thing as making more money. Because human beings are risk-averse, saying you can cut costs takes their eye off the initial target and puts it on yours. Harmless, right? Effective? Absolutely.

Second, if it's better for you to round up, round up. If it's better for you to round down, round down. As a salesperson, this is a fabulous tactic because you can always hedge performance just enough to get to "yes!" When you interview for your next job, tell the interviewer you're the top salesperson. Tell them you are a great team member and you have vast experience selling as a team - even if you only have been on your own or a lousy team member. If the information is hard to verify, manipulate it to make you look great. You can also manipulate stats and data, especially if it's your stats and your own data. Who are they to question your stats and your own data? Inflate, make things look 10% better than they really are – whatever it takes to get the sale!

Finally, manipulate perceived outcomes. If you can move the goalposts, move them. If the customer says they need 100%, show them all the benefits of only getting 97%. Set big expectations from the first meeting all the way to final negotiations. Then trim those expectations down. "Mr. Customer, you said you'd be delighted if you got A, B, C, and D. After talking, isn't it true that you'd only be happy with A and B?" Then work them down to A. Disguise those expectations in the veil of, "We will grow with you. Let's start small and grow." Land and expand. All that crap. It's perfect manipulation.

If you can manipulate, you can get anyone to sign a contract. If you can do this to make people buy something that they don't need, then congratulations, you're a shitty salesperson.

LIVE ON PLAN B

Shitty Nick, a real-life *Dr. Jekyll and Mr. Hyde,* sometimes made the radical decision to live on Plan B. Why? It fed his irrational neurosis and at the same time made him look like a "big picture" kind of guy. Aren't you "big picture?" That's real value to a company; a sales person who's looking out for anything and everything that could go wrong.

The feelings you will get from constantly worrying about what could, or what should, or what can and developing plans around those hypothetical questions is a wonderful way not to handle the tasks at-hand. It's a great thing to do because you will look busy. Coworkers will see you as the "thinker." Don't you want to show people that you're thoughtful?

The present is today, but shouldn't you worry about what you're doing tomorrow? If you're like me and are always planning, you'll always be working. You'll be able to go to your manager with lots of questions. Sure, these questions may not matter today, but they are questions that show that you think about the big picture. You'll demonstrate that you're the type of person who looks to the future!

Always thinking about the future and what could happen might even give you the title as Company Visionary. Don't you want to be ready for when the proverbial meteor hits? Do today's relationships ultimately matter? Shouldn't you be cultivating the relationships of tomorrow? Need a great excuse for why you didn't make more sales calls today? Throw out this gem: "I was white-boarding some ideas of what we would do if we lost our best customers, or if we lost our best suppliers." Try it, see what happens! Spouting answers to questions like that will make your manager look at you in a totally different light. How can you meet a problem the right way if you spend no time thinking about it?

What virtue is there focusing on the task at hand and today's problems when there could potentially be a bigger problem tomorrow? The best part about this approach is that it gives you the opportunity to create all sorts of scenarios, no matter how improbable they are, and put up real concrete blocks to getting done what you need to get done today. It's beautiful. You can show everyone how busy you are without getting a thing done, and still getting paid your base salary.

Another benefit to always thinking about Plan B is that it stops you from becoming overly committed to your product and company. Remember that story of Cortés burning his ships when they got to the new world? That was quite the motivation for his group. Who needs that? What could you possibly gain from going all in? By giving all your time, energy and effort? I'll tell you: smaller territories, shorter timelines, and higher quotas. That's your reward.

There's always a chance your company has a plan B for you, so why shouldn't you have a Plan B for them? Keep your eye on Plan B, and it's a guarantee, you'll always be a shitty salesperson.

DON'T LISTEN

Shitty Nick knew that talking was better than listening. Prospects needed to be told what to do, what to buy, how much to pay, and when to buy it. Aren't you in charge of the situation? Commanders don't listen, they tell. Be the general.

Listening takes work. Listening means processing. Listening means thinking. Listening means adapting. Listening means acting. So exhausting! Customers buy on price. Whatever their concern is, whatever their objection is, it doesn't matter. Remember, customers only buy on price. Listening to them drone on about how they haven't been able to solve a particular problem or exploit opportunities after buying your product is secondary if you're not the cheapest.

How do you go through a sales meeting and look like you're engaged when you're not? First, never bring a pen and paper. Why? Now you can keep eye contact! Respond with phrases like, "I completely understand" and "That makes total sense" or "Exactly what I was thinking!" or "You are not alone in that experience." Fill your responses with fillers like "uh-huh," "oh yes," and "Absolutely!" Phrases like "Not a problem" and "Easily solvable" will make your customer think that you understand what they're trying to say. Do you? Do you care? Heck no. You're just waiting to show the price (and they're waiting to hear it).

When the customer has babbled about their critical business issues, outlined various pain points, and revealed to you what will make them happy, simply offer your product at the cheapest price. If they come back at you and say that your product might not do what they think it means to, you tell them: "If I hear you right you need it to do X, Y & Z. Trust me it will do X, Y & Z." If you don't listen, how can you be responsible for the results?

Listening might mean more homework, but if you don't do more homework, you won't have to face a reality that you or you, your product, or company aren't in the best interest of the customer. Bad! Your job, as a salesperson, is not to find out what's best for the customer. Your job is to get prospects to buy your product.

Don't believe it? READ YOUR JOB DESCRIPTION. There isn't a single line about doing what's best for the customer. Why in the world would you do any behavior that made the customer the priority? That's insane. If it's best for the customer, it might not be for you. If they don't sign on your contract, will they pay your bills?

Not listening will help you focus on your message and you won't need to listen very hard to prospects telling you: "You're a shitty salesperson!!!" Congratulations.

DON'T MAKE COLD CALLS

Despite all the talk, Shitty Nick avoided cold calls. They're a source of immediate rejection and unless it's a "976" number, can you really make a connection?

This might be the most obvious piece of advice: take it to heart! The idea that putting yourself out there either through phone calls, emails, networking, door to door knocking, business social media, you name it; it is such an important activity to avoid if you want to be a shitty salesperson. In a general sense, sales is a "numbers game." It's a fact. If you are actively out there with a regular schedule of phone calls, various email techniques, social media techniques and things like that, then eventually you are going to find somebody at some time who's willing to buy your product for the price you have listed. Blind squirrels find nuts.

When you regularly make cold calls, send emails and connect through social media, you are acting on a premeditated routine. The results of which will give you some predictability, data, and help you forecast what your results should be. It will also highlight areas where you might be having some challenges. None of these are the mark of a shitty salesperson. The total result of these behaviors will be a position of constant discomfort. You'll be forced to think about your process and then see how it relates to your internal and external competition. What could be more painful than learning the truth about your pipeline?

Cold calling will force you to experience more rejection. What kind of life is a life full of rejection? And what if part of your calling routine means listening to your calls? How painful is that? You'll find out just how ridiculous you sound on the phone. You'll involuntarily cringe at the words you use. The tone and timbre of your voice will drive you crazy. There will be a permanent record of your inability to influence somebody.

Then what? Is your manager going to use that as a perfect example of what not to do and set you up as the laughingstock of the company? Yes! Making you look bad also makes them look good for being able to identify just how bad you are. Why in the world would you give them that opportunity? Do you get a commission bonus for that? Hell no!

I get it. In your job, you must prospect, but don't do it with any methodology. Forget any testing, certainly, don't record and review. Never try to follow up with someone who said no to help understand why the prospect wouldn't go further with you on the phone call. Rather, if your quota is 20 phone calls, make 20 phone calls. Then go to the bar and talk about how stupid customers are. You'll feel a lot better.

Shitty Nick did so little prospecting that it's safe to say: fewer calls sped Shitty Nick to his status of Shitty Salesperson - it can do the same for you.

DON'T DO HOMEWORK

Shitty Nick was a shitty student. No homework; still got a B+. What's the problem? More time to play games, drink beer, and chase girls. A charmed life, indeed!

Ignoring homework seems elementary, but homework is a dangerous tool that changes the entire landscape of the selling process. Homework will put the pieces of the puzzle together. Homework reveals motives. Homework helps you (not) repeat history. It's like playing with fire.

First, remember homework complicates the sales process. If, in the course of doing homework on your customer, you find out a very important piece of information that might not put your company in the best light, what do you do next? You've potentially shot yourself in the foot. See how dangerous homework is?! Always ask yourself: is your job to do what's best for the customer or your company? Who writes your commission check?

Your job is to hunt and kill. Homework reveals reasons why your customer won't even consider your solution...especially if this is the second or third attempt as an organization. Crumple up the past and throw it out. What good is old information? You need a clean slate. You don't need to be bogged down with the baggage of sales past.

Second, homework tells you the mistakes other people have made. How can you learn from mistakes you'd never make? What's an immutable fact about homework? Homework begets more homework. You can't rest on one piece of information. You're beholden to the whole story. Once you put the pieces together, what do you have to do? Put it in the CRM! Major mistake!

What happens when the account gets transferred from you? Then your co-worker, who is also your competitor, gets that information and earns the sale instead of you because your manager allows a discount (because he needs his bonus)! It happens all the time. An account gets pulled because the sales rep didn't have enough time, or the decision maker wasn't correct, or something changed in the marketplace. The next salesperson gets the account and boom – closed! Is that fair to the original rep? Nope! Homework is baggage. Go into your calls with a clean slate and no pre-conceived notions from previous facts.

Third, there's no point in knowing account history because it doesn't apply. Why? Customers only care about price, so homework wastes your time. It forces you to get even more responsible about the sales process. With more responsibility comes more ownership of everything that happens – all because of the knowledge you know. It can all be taken away from you in the blink of an eye, given to somebody else, and really, the customer doesn't care.

Why would the customer care that you have a common bond? Why would the customer care that you have a common history? Why would the customer care that you have some insights into their industry? Why would the customer care that you can challenge their assumptions? Why does the customer care about any of that? They don't. Customers only care about price. They know exactly what your product can do – they want to know the lowest price you'll settle for.

Tell your customer the dog ate your homework, and you'll be valedictorian of shitty salespeople.

DISPARAGE SUPPORT STAFF

Shitty Nick ensured Support Staff knew their place – below, supporting him. That's why they're called "support staff." The value of Support Staff is 100% utilitarian. Don't believe it? Read on.

There is a reason you're the salesperson, and they are not. You are organized, detail-oriented, and always charming. You are aggressive and never rude. You excel at juggling the nuances of business and never make mistakes. Beyond that, you are the reason that people say "Yes!" to your company. Without salespeople, there is no business, and you are no exception. With that as the backdrop, how should you treat sales support staff? Any way you want. If you want to be nice, be nice. If you want to be mean, be mean. But really, be mean. Here are some more ideas.

Always be inconsistent. Keep staff on their toes. Don't ever give them an idea of what version of "you" will show up today. They are experts at walking on eggshells, so hurt feelings on their part are not your concern. Never view them as a partner or collaborator. Their job is to help you execute and to put out your fires. They have a job description, and they are compensated based on their ability to complete the job.

Nowhere does it say that the salespeople the support staff works with are obligated to be nice or helpful. Save those behaviors for when you really need them. Don't waste them on support staff. They are not collaborators with you. They are worker bees. Never give more credit than they deserve. Short of them getting the meeting, or making the connection, or having the customer sign on the dotted line - they should receive no public accolades from you. If they want that kind of attention and glory, then they should sit down at a phone and make a call.

If you can impart a sense of tribalism between the sales team and the support staff, do it. What you'll create is a bond between members of the support staff team. You've now built their bridges, and they can lean on each other. If they have anything to complain about, they can complain to each other. It's not your job to learn about and fix their problems.

Finally, don't ever share a commission with support staff. Workers are due their wages. You have your agreement with the company; they have theirs. What's fair is fair. Plus, what do you think would happen if you started sharing your commission with your support staff? You know what will happen - they will feel like they're members of the sales team! They will feel invested and start to share opinions and ideas. Who wants that? What do they know? They don't have the training or the experience you have, why should they get the reward?

If you want to be a shitty salesperson, make support staff feel like the tools they are...and you'll be known as the tool you are.

EMBRACE BAD BUSINESS

Shitty Nick knew that *any* business was better than *no* business. You can have a check and a problem or no check and no problem. What would you rather choose?

You work so hard to get all the business that you can, why in the world would you refuse business or refer business to a co-worker or even a competitor? You would much rather own a problem customer than just own the problem of having no customer.

Isn't your primary allegiance to your pocketbook? How could you benefit from helping someone else out? Who cares if you don't have the best solution for your customer? Buyer beware; it's the prospect's job to evaluate who the best provider is, not yours. What would a prospect think if you told them that you're not the best solution but that your willing to help them find someone who is? They would think you're nuts. In my opinion, there is no such thing as bad business. If it makes you money or could make you money, you should put as much time, energy and effort and resources into it as possible.

As soon as you start digging into what the customer needs, you might find out all sorts of tidbits that could make you question whether to write the business. Warts like past payment problems or implementation challenges might pop up. Big deal, they have a problem, and you're there to sell them a solution that (may) solve it.

What's the worst that could happen? A customer that saps all your energy? That from the start you're set up for failure? The realization you've bitten off more than you can chew? Does the new customer pull time away from other more valuable customers? Maybe, but you never know until you find out. And don't most of these problems fall to Account Managers and the Customer Service team? Let them deal with the problem. You solved the first one: getting new business.

Don't pass along business. Take as much as you can. Good business, bad business, tough business, easy business. Business that makes you money. Business that doesn't make you money. Business that takes time. Business that gives you time take it all, never refer it. It's your business. Take it!

Remember, if you want to be a shitty sales person, go after shitty business.

AVOID: WHO, WHAT, WHY, AND HOW

Shitty Nick avoided complex question that started with: who, what, why, and how. Why? Those questions mean work – work beyond your perfectly-executed robotic presentation. Those words force customers to think and you to respond. That's not fun or easy and if anything, it can delay signatures.

You want resolution. "No" is better than "I don't know, call me back in 6 months." If you want to force a decision, avoid these four questions:

1. Then who?
2. Then what?
3. Then why?
4. Then how?

Why don't you want to ask these questions? What should be the first question you avoid? "***Who?!***" Every sale is complex. You must deal with several different decision makers or decision-making personas. If you want to slow down the sales process, never ask the question, "then who?" Because if you ask the question, you'll find out that you are not as close to the sale as you assumed. And you always want to make your manager think that you're saddled right up next to the decision maker. "Then who" screws that up.

By asking, "Then who?" you open yourself up to more work, changing your value proposition, and tightening up your message across buying personas. All you want as a salesperson is to get to "yes" or "no" as fast as possible. If you ask, "Then who?" you're going to lengthen the sales process and do more work!

The second dangerous question to ask is, "Then what?" By asking "Then what?" you're bombarded with everything your customer must do to say yes. You might get an insight into their motive. You might make them believe you care about what happens to them. Do you? No! You care about your commission. That's why you're in sales. "Then what?" is code for "tell me what else is involved." But do you want to know all the aspects of the decision? Never worked for Shitty Nick.

The third dangerous question is, "Then why?" "Then why?" opens the can of excuse worms. "Then why?" might reveal what's wrong with you, your product, your service, your pricing, or your terms. Why would you want to know what's wrong? Aren't you supposed to focus on what's right? If you ask, "Then why?" you might get your feelings hurt. Your ego might get bruised. You might see that you didn't have a chance in the first place. All that information is going to do is drag you down and reduce your commission.

The final question, piggybacks on the third question, and it is, "Then how?" This is the ultimate question because it puts the customer on the spot about how the two of you move forward. How's it asked?

"Then how do we solve this problem?"
"Then how do we get the other stakeholders to the table?"
"Then how do we get everyone else to buy in?"

If you're asking all these questions, ***then how*** are you going to get to the bar for happy hour? Sales is about doing the least amount of work for the most amount of profit. These questions bring out the complexity of the sale and stand to reduce your commission significantly. "Then how?" is code for: "Please give me more work to help you solve this problem even though I am only going to get paid the same amount." If you're going to avoid any of these questions, "Then how?" is the one to avoid.

Skip these questions, and then you'll know who, what, why, and how you became a shitty salesperson.

BE THE VICTIM

Shitty Nick knew the one person he could become to manipulate managers, mislead customers, and abuse support staff: *the victim.* Victims get rewards and pity. *Victims* have lots of resources – use them!

How do you become a sales victim? Develop your Excuse Machine in such a way that other people feel your pain.

You can say things like:

- They didn't like my sex
- They didn't like my color
- They didn't like my religion
- They didn't like me because of my culture
- They didn't like me because of my university
- They didn't like me because of my politics

Parlay these lines into more unverifiable events:

- They wouldn't answer the phone.
- They wouldn't give me a meeting.
- They wouldn't sit down at the negotiating table

The best excuse is "They wouldn't give me a fair shot." Isn't that what you deserve? A fair shot, a chance to lay it all out on the line to highlight your value proposition, to put your price down on pencil and paper and be told "yes!" If you can highlight somebody's unfair behavior, you might look like a reasonable person and better yet: someone bound by the constraints of the situation and not your inability.

People will view you as someone who tried to do more but couldn't. Not because you didn't want to do more but because you weren't able to do more. You've earned a second chance. You shouldn't be fired; you should have a shot at winning business from another prospect. The blame game is great to play if you are on a team and you need to get above that 20% or what-

ever that number is that doesn't get fired.
Put it all together with lines:

- Boss, I would have crushed my quota, but they didn't like my more relaxed approach to the situation.
- Boss, I would have gotten my quota, but the decision maker was a lesbian, and I'm a straight male.
- Boss, I would have gotten my sales, but they don't respect women, it's a good old boys' network.

While it may take a bit of creativity, learning how to become the victim in any circumstance is vital to you keeping your job for as long as possible. Shift blame to the errors of the customer, support staff, or to your sales manager. If you can do it, you'll see how fun it is to be the victim and to be a shitty salesperson.

MIX-UP IMPORTANT AND URGENT

Shitty Nick will tell you: mix-up important vs. urgent and reap the benefits of lots of work and few rewards.

Pay attention! Developing this skill helps you look busy even when you're not. First, let's define it. Important are those things that need to get done, and urgent are those things that need to get done ***now***.

If you remember that definition, no matter what activity you have in front of you, you can always answer: "Is this important or is this urgent?" Does this need to get done or does this need to get done now? All you need to do is take those tasks which need to get done now and put them off until later. Conversely, take tasks that aren't time sensitive and make them a priority - pushing the urgent until a later, more convenient time (for you).

Say you need to get a proposal done by end-of-day. It's urgent, but should put it off? Yes, push off what's urgent and do what's important. You can continue to work on it but finishing it and delivering it off to the customer can wait. You can replace an urgent activity with an important activity like cold calling, going to an unnecessary meeting, or taking time to talk to talk your sales manager so you can build a stronger bond.

All those things are important, but if you make those important things urgent, you can put off the urgent things. If you're always working on urgent things, you'll never have time to work on the important things. See? Everything becomes urgent! Either way, you're busy, and it looks like you're constantly working on *something*. When you juxtapose the important and urgent, you end up in a wonderful state of paralysis, but you still look busy!

The nice part about urgency is that you can get to define it. It may be important to set a schedule for prospecting, but it's urgent that you make a follow-up call or some other activity. Now you have an opportunity to turn what was important into something that's urgent and what's urgent into something that's important - the cycle repeats itself!

How do you know if you're on track? If you ever feel like you've been working a lot but don't have much to show for it, you're probably on track for understanding this lesson and mastering the important and urgent task of becoming a shitty salesperson.

LIVE IN BLACK & WHITE

Shitty Nick lived in a binary world. It's fabulous because problems and solutions appear simple and easy to solve. Anybody who says that the world is grey is just afraid to admit it's black and white.

Yes or no. One or zero. On or off. Live the phrase: keep it simple, Stupid. If everything is BW, then every question and answer is simple. Do you have the prospect's attention? Are they interested? Can they make decisions? Will they take buying actions? If you live your sales life in a binary world, you can ignore all the complexities of a sale. You get to give simple answers to your customer and manager. You won't get bogged down things like critical thinking. Feed your Excuse Machine with yes/no answers and you will always have a difinitive answer.

The best way to view buying/selling decisions through the BW lens is to ignore the fact that every buyer is always on a "buying spectrum." Buyers are always in position to say yes or no. Even after a customer makes their decision, they're not off the spectrum. Haven't you seen it? A buyer signs on the dotted line and the next day is given a different solution (how could it possibly be better???), and you get the Email/call saying, "Sorry Joe-bag-of-Donuts, we're going in a different direction."

What's this spectrum look like? Draw an arrow pointing to the left and label it "holding." Then draw an arrow next to it pointing to the right and label it "buying." The closer prospects are to the end of each arrowhead, the more committed they are to a decision. Most of the time, buyers are somewhere in the middle - even right after a purchase. If you're paying attention to this spectrum, you might be able to take advantage of "buyer's remorse" but you're not because living in a BW sales world means you don't have the time for these complexities!

It takes a lot of effort to confidently be one thing or the other, but it simplifies a lot of decisions. You won't get bogged down with questions like "then what" or "what if" or "what would" that abound in a "grey" world.

If you think of a customer as someone who's buying or isn't, you know exactly what you need to do with them and with your time. You've got a quota to meet and going back to your manager without a definitive answer will make you look like an idiot.

Embrace the B/W attitude and it will be as plain as black and white to your customers that you are a shitty salesperson.

RUPTURE RAPPORT

Shitty Nick ignored rapport and you should too. Why? Rapport is BS. Does any buyer care if you have areas of common interest? Prospects only care about price and problems - or the solving or *their* problems. If that's what you believe, you're already on track to rupturing rapport.

Rapport is about finding common ground and requires you to empathize with the pain your prospect experiences or the pleasure they *want to* experience. You don't have time for that. You've got features and benefits to cover, terms to outline, and price to negotiate. Go with your gut. If the prospect likes your solution, he's into you. That's real rapport.

Skip the pleasantries and jump to:

"What's in your budget?"
"How soon do you want to take delivery?"
"We offer special financing only available today, would you like to use it?"
"By month-end, delivery is free delivery, want to buy today?"
"Waiting on your income tax return?" (it's a gutsy question and can pay off bigtime)

When you rupture rapport, it makes it easier to go for the jugular. Prospects love that level of directness. Who cares if buyers can feel your arrogance? Maybe *they* are wrong, not you? Jump into your pitch, trust me, they'll appreciate it.

Here are the little steps to rupturing rapport

- Don't worry about acting nice; customers are interested in price
- Leave your smile at the door. People feel awkward when you smile
- Trap people with your body. Physically put them in a corner, stand straight-on, and don't let them escape. Women love this

- Don't think of questions beforehand, let the conversation flow. No plan > a bad plan
- Never develop powerful opening statements because it's impossible for you to impress a decision maker in 30 seconds
- Stay on-point too long and don't offer a subsequent follow-up. You're here to sell today. Right now. ABC.
- In the unfortunate event you have to follow-up, don't do it with questions. Give them canned ideas with a cheap price.

Here are the big steps to rupturing rapport

- Don't dig into the past to understand the problem
- Never ask: "How?" and "Then what?"
- Ignore how people outside the decision are affected by you, your product and service
- Never invite customers to be part of the product development process
- Don't let customers know other people in your organization
- Never try to connect decision-makers with other decision-makers
- Don't show customers new business opportunities
- Make the "less important" feel the least important
- Highlight how YOU are your customer's success
- Forget being nice, magnanimous, gracious, and fun

If you follow these steps, you'll never have to worry about whether you've built rapport, you'll have ruptured any rapport and stood out as a shitty salesperson.

PUSH, PUSH, PUSH, PUSH, & PUSH

Shitty Nick never stopped pushing... pushing prospects, managers, and coworkers. People are lazy. They're like donkeys: if you don't kick'm, they won't move.

If you don't push as hard as you possibly can for sale, there's no way it will happen. Don't relent. Don't give customers space to think. Don't let them understand all the options. The options aren't important. The only option that matters is *your* option.

There are two great ways to always be pushing: FUD and FOMO. If you can put every conversation in terms of fear, uncertainty, and doubt, then you can make prospects uncomfortable enough to act! You can scare them into action through FOMO. Use FOMO to create time constraints, mythical savings, and unnecessary terms. People only buy to remove pain - use these techniques to FUD or FOMO prospects into the sale!

Tell prospects "every day you wait, the more expensive it is to take away the pain!" You've got a quota to meet! That's your problem that needs to go away. If you're not pushing your customers towards a decision, you're wasting time and money. Aren't you in sales to make money ASAP? Don't you have FUD and FOMO over your commission?

Your boss and your boss' boss always push you. You must push the customer. That's how the relationship works. Don't be afraid to let prospects know how important the sale is to you. If you don't push prospects, they will stall or spend ***your*** money somewhere else. Tell customers that their time-wasting is your money wasting. Tell them you want to help, but you can't help if they won't say "yes!"

Be sure to tell customers that you need to close them and that the transaction needs to close because if there's one thing that people love most, it's being told that they're being closed. Don't be shy, be honest. They know what's going on. You're selling them. You can't ask for the business, you've got to demand the business or somebody else will.

Remember: if you don't know when to stop being pushy, you'll never stop being a shitty salesperson.

DON'T READ THESE BOOK

Shitty Nick never read sales books – why? He knew it all, so do you. Read the list and move on.

"Think and Grow Rich" - Napoleon Hill. What could a book about the power of thought, written in 1937 by a guy most considered a fraud and who failed at building several businesses teach you about how to succeed?

"The Little Red Book of Selling" - Jeffrey Gitomer. With ideas like "reducing the risk of buying" and offering "value first" as opposed to "price first" Jeffrey tries to convince you that selling is easy. What could the guy who wrote the best-selling sales book of all time know?

"How to Win Friends and Influence People" - Dale Carnegie. He expects us to remember and address a person by their first name? And how can you not ridicule, insult, and antagonize the competition? All that and a lot more "wisdom" in that book.

"The 10X Rule" - Grant Cardone. You work hard enough; do you need this self-made millionaire telling you to work harder?

The Bible - God. Someone, please show me one story in this collection of books that has anything to do with persuasion. Good luck.

"The Challenger Sale." - Matthew Dixon / Brent Adamson. There's no guide to selling big, complex, enterprise sales - it's a crapshoot. Plus, as if you can challenge the assumptions of your customer... aren't they always right?

"The 7 Habits of Highly Effective People" - Stephen R. Covey. Nothing but a litany of activities you as a salesperson don't have time for because if you're not closing, you're dying.

"Thinkertoys" - Michael Mickhalko. There's only one solution to every sales problem: price. Thinking is wasting time.

"Agile Selling" - Jill Konrath. Can women sell? Didn't think so. It's hard to believe buyers are on a spectrum instead of buying or not. You only want to talk to people who are buying today.
"The Psychology of Sales" - Brian Tracy. Just like there was no spoon in The Matrix, there's no psychology in sales. People want, or they don't. What's to figure out in that equation?

Books are dangerous weapons that shouldn't be used willy-nilly. Books hold the potential to reshape your mind and impact your behaviors. What does that have to do with hitting your quota?

If there's one takeaway from this list, it should be: stay an illiterate salesperson, and you'll always be a shitty salesperson.

SEPARATE SALES AND SERVICE

Shitty Nick once saw a sign in front of a car dealership. One sign with an arrow pointing left said "SALES" and a sign right next to it, pointing right, said "SERVICE." Perfect. That's exactly how it should be. There's no crying in baseball, and there's no room for service in sales. Sounds tricky, but here's the math.

Sales and service are very different. Sales is what happens *before* the customer buys and service is what happens *after* the customer buys. They require vastly different skill sets to execute and should never mix together - they're like water and oil.

As a salesperson, you're a hunter or farmer. You need to go out and bring home the bacon or till the field until it produces. Your job is to prospect, build pipelines, move the ball down the field, and get people to say "yes!" Sales drive services, not the other way around. Your "sale" is your service - you're doing a service to someone in need, and they're paying you for it. They should be grateful for your call.

Think about service - isn't service a reaction? Doesn't service usually cost **you** money? Fair to say service is a time-sink? Service usually happens because of a problem the customer encountered that wasn't your fault. Service means you're in the business of fixing things and offering restitution (money back, extended contracts, etc.). Service means dealing with shit.

When sales and service are separated, there's no tension. Everyone has their responsibility and stays in their lane. Can you imagine what would happen if a customer service representative was stepping on your toes? They're not the *relationship person* - you are! Let the car salesman sell the cars and the technician service them. Pass off customers to "account managers" whenever possible. Don't bother reading customer surveys - those people aren't ever happy.

Service always tries to get in the business of sales, but that's a recipe for disaster. Below are simple examples of keeping these two activities far apart – can't do the same for your business?

- Be the car salesman who sells cars but won't promote the service department.
- Be the jeweler who offers the "best price" but nickel-and-dimes over repairs.
- Be the insurance agent who only calls after the disaster.
- Be the salesperson who promises 24/7 service but only when convenient for you.

When you start to split sales from service in your professional life, it becomes easier to do it in your personal life!

- Be the husband who's only "there" after your wife nags
- Be the father who thinks that yelling at his kid doubles as quality time because you're teaching lessons
- Be the son who only calls home for bail money
- Be the friend who makes friendship transactional

Sales and service aren't a match made in Heaven - they're a divorce that lives in Hell. Service rides sales coattails to legitimacy, and it's your job to stop it.

You sell, let someone else serve, and you'll separate yourself from the crowd as a shitty salesperson.

EMBRACE DESTRUCTIVE VICES

Shitty Nick didn't buy much, but he did make a few purchases from the "vice" department. If you want to be a shitty salesperson, he's got a coupon you can use for a discount.

Vices are awesome because they help you live in a constant state of excitement; chasing adrenaline, forgetting about problems, and hiding from the realities of life. Vices are easy to pick up and can have a dramatic impact on your sales business. Vices, if left unchecked, will take over your life and it'll be a wild ride 'til the end. Here's the tip of the "Viceberg" and quick-start-guide to get you hooked.

Let's say you just got a big commission check. What should you do? Go to the casino and try to parlay it on the craps table. If it works, you're paid in all cash; you double your money, awesome. If it doesn't work out, you have a new motivation for the next day. It's possible that you will sell a bit harder, more forcefully, but whatever. That's the price you pay for a little bit of fun at the casino.

Sex is a great way to ruin your sales career because you can bring sex into every equation. You will look at people differently. You will think of people differently. People become objects - objects for you to use for your immediate satisfaction. You wouldn't think that it would affect your sales, but fewer things have had a more destructive set of toxic consequences on business than sex.

Alcohol is the salesperson's best friend. It's always there, easily accessible, and relatively cheap. The best part? It's socially acceptable. Salespeople are expected to get wasted so if you're in sales and not getting wasted on a regular basis; you're doing it wrong! Alcohol helps you break the ice. It makes you likable. It makes you more attractive to opposite. It helps you take chances and throw caution to the wind. Drink. Drink a lot. Shots. Beer. Wine. Doesn't matter - if you've can drink, drink.

Nothing else so easy to intake that can have quite the impact.

If you let your vices get the best of you, the impact on your sales career is too big to describe. Throw caution to the wind. Don't worry. The result will be your addiction to life as a shitty salesperson.

BELIEVE YOU'RE IRREPLACEABLE

Shitty Nick was a limited resource. As much as managers wanted, they couldn't duplicate him. So are you: one-of-a-kind. Who or what could take your spot? You're the focal point of business – do your thing, you'll be rewarded accordingly.

Nothing happens without the sale, and the sale doesn't happen without the salesperson. See? You're the most important person in the company. Why would anyone fire you? You go out and bring home the bacon. You're the hunter. You're the producer that feeds the village. You should have latitude to do, think, and say what you feel about the current state of the business. Unless somebody else will make a cold call, do the meeting, and close the business, they should shut up.

If you make quota, shouldn't your job be safe? The more you beat your quota, the safer your job is. At that point, you are the BSD of the office. This allows you to be late, rude, inconsiderate, arrogant, and greedy. You're untouchable. You know it, your co-workers know it, and your boss knows it. Your boss can tolerate your toxicity or make less money. What do you think she will choose?

Maybe you're not the top salesperson, but there is no way that a company is ever going to get rid of business development reps. Can a robot do as good of a job as you can? Will Watson replace you? Never! Does your company have the creativity necessary to drive ready-to-buy inbound leads? Any reasonable salesperson is a terrible asset to lose; managers know this. Could AI be as good as you on the phone? Never!

Because you're irreplaceable, there's a certain joy in being able to do the bare minimum. It's a big risk for a manager to fire someone who barely makes their quota. Why would you do any more work than necessary? If you are pretty much guaranteed to do 100%, it's a risky proposition for managers to get rid of you, train somebody new, and hope that they get 105% or 110%

of what you've been doing. Don't believe it? When was the last time management fired the middle 50%? If you can't be at the top, be in the middle.

Read the chapter on sandbagging to perfect this tactic. That's the best part about the belief of not being replaceable. Whether you're an average salesperson or a great salesperson, with this belief, you can always be a shitty salesperson.

IGNORE OTHER BUSINESS DISCIPLINES

Shitty Nick knew sales. Why should he (or you) know anything else? Don't believe it? Go down this thought-experiment.

The dirty truth: as a salesperson, you don't have the luxury of learning about product development, management, financing, and accounting, marketing, human resources, legal and regulatory issues, operations, and people management. Does any of that help you make a cold call? Do those build your pipeline? Do they build your referral business? Never did for Shitty Nick

Some people might call those areas "business disciplines" – they're noise. If you risk of mixing disciplines ("discipline is used as loosely as possible), you'll find out all the complex issues that go into making a purchasing decision. Said another way, you will quickly identify all the areas that prolong the sales cycle.

You don't have that luxury. There's no way a multiple-disciplinary approach to sales can help you get to "yes!" faster. If you sell a solution to an operations problem, why put it in terms of people management? If you offer a finance solution, why frame it in the science of supply chain management? If you sell a product that reduces costs, why address revenue issues? The competition doesn't do that. Why would you?

The customer expects and wants conventional thoughts and ideas. If you're busy tying together all the other aspects of her business (as it relates to your widget), you risk the customer getting bogged down in lots of details and thinking through all the implications of their purchase. You don't want them to think; you want them to buy.

When it comes to sales, both from the buyer and seller's perspective, ignorance is bliss. If you start connecting dots, you risk customers realizing you're not the best solution. Put yourself in the buyer's shoes and ask yourself if you would want to know all the details before you make a purchase? Buyers only buy because they are in pain. Anything that reduces pain, ASAP, even if there's a better solution elsewhere, is something no rational buyer would buy.

That's why it's dangerous to know too much about your product. As the salesperson, your job is to simplify everything for the customer. Could the buyer be impressed if you knew exactly how the coding of a software solution worked because you had a strong working knowledge of JavaScript, or Ruby, or Python? Maybe. What will the buyer think when you use your legislative knowledge to talk about how new laws will impact their pipeline? They'll probably think you're some policy wonk. And what if you used your experience and knowledge in Lean Manufacturing to go beyond Six Sigma and tie it to business intelligence? The customer will think you belong in some B-School. Your nuanced knowledge isn't as important as your price.

Prospects don't want a product nerd, prospects want smooth talkers - people that will make them feel good. Is it important that a medical device salesperson has a legitimate working knowledge of physiology, or anatomy, or chemistry, or biology? It's a mystery. Haven't you sold things backed by a technology that you didn't know squat about?

Focus on features and benefits. Nail product and pricing. Let those "solution sellers" and "360-degree Trusted Advisors" take the big risks. You don't have time for any of that or any other business discipline – you're focus is on being a shitty salesperson.

FOCUS ON PROFIT

Shitty Nick knew that there was one goal in business: maximizing profit. That's why he was in sales, how about you?

Nothing is more important than profit to a shitty salesperson. It' so important that every activity you do should drive profit. Pay no attention that the fact that profit is a byproduct of a variety of business activities. Confused? Keep reading.

Profit is the outcome of good product design, channel management, the ability to engage a variety of probable purchasers, a relatable story, strategic marketing techniques, a complimentary referral system, an easy purchasing process, and superior service that drives loyalty not customer satisfaction (the lowest rung on the ladder). Getting to profit requires a combination of guts, the ability to pick up the phone and make the connection and grit, the drive to press-on after rejection.

The actualization of these activities drives profitability, but it means that your eye can never be on the profitability ball. How can you close without thinking about profit? You must focus on two simple questions: does this person or company make me money and how fast do you make it? You have no room for asking yourself a question like, "Is this purchase a good thing for the customer and my company?" You can't give any oxygen to the question, "is what I am selling ethical, or does what I sell improve the world around me or the world for other people?"

When profit is the primary goal, you can look at any problem clearly and justify any action. The best part about this attitude is that it is insanely contagious. Your drive and hunger for profit can change the behaviors of your co-workers, your managers and even of the executive team.

That's the beauty of focusing in on profit. The street runs both ways. Everybody can learn to accept any business practice so long as profit takes primacy. Who cares about brand and market share or reputation? Certainly not you when you're making money, why should anyone else?

If you've got the guts and the grit to focus on profit, someday you'll be known as the shit(tiest salesperson).

DON'T COVER YOUR BASES

Shitty Nick hated baseball. Long, technical, and ever-changing. Cover your quota, not your bases.

Before I begin, I confess: I didn't think of this one. Peter shared this idea. He fired me. Thanks, Peter. Sales have never been the same.

Baseball has a lot to teach about sales – but at its basic level, think of the four bases in a baseball diamond. Assign first base to the *User* persona, the second base to the company *Champion*, the third base to the *Purse Strings* or financial decision maker (think CFO), and home plate is the *Ultimate* decision maker (CEO/ Owner/P&L/etc.). Every buying decision needs to cover all four bases, so here's who they are and how to get called "out" at each one.

The User is the person who actively uses the product or service. If you have or if you can create disharmony or tension between you and first base, it's a guarantee the sale will go nowhere. The company might say yes to start, but if the user isn't happy, the sale will fail.

The Champion is the mover, shaker, and dreamer in an organization. Often, they're the person who is trying to make a splash, who is trying to disrupt the status quo, who wants to move up and show how important they are. Think "classic MBA with zero experience." They may not use the product, they certainly don't have the purse strings, and they are not the final decision maker, but they are a major influencer in the decision to proceed. Some people might call this person the pleasure person - not the person who is trying to remove pain specifically, but the person who is trying to do something big. They could also be the pain button. A good way to crash a sale is not to engage the Champion. They are the person who can have conversations with other decision makers that you aren't allowed to talk to. Champions know certain details or have motivations necessary to make the sale happen. Ignore them.

Third base is the purse strings (CFO). Just like baseball, the triple is the hardest hit to hit, and the CFO is the hardest person to convince. How do you screw things up with the purse strings? Simple, talk about cost and price. Avoid the words "return on investment." Highlight how the payback period can extend out. Never talk about efficiency improvements that save money. Pay no attention to how your product will increase revenue or decrease cost AND drive profitability. Be vague with pricing and the renewal structure or ongoing cost.

Finally, never cover home plate: the Ultimate decision maker. The Ultimate decision maker considers all the ideas and perceptions about your value from first, second, and third base. There seems to be no better way to kill a sale than not engage the Ultimate decision maker. Don't make him a priority. Don't help him put the pieces of the puzzle together; make him do it on his own. Home plate is the executive, shouldn't they be able to figure out your value proposition?

Secret tip: want to really screw things up? Pit first base against third base, second base against first, home plate against second base, etc. Don't create allies, create division. The ensuing mess will kill any sale.

If you avoid covering your bases, you will soon be playing the cleanup position on the team of shitty salespeople.

DUMP YOUR DATABASE

Shitty Nick hated his CRM and hot-sheets. You should too. Databases are worthless. Databases are a waste of time and a tool used by management to keep you down.

As a salesperson, you've got all your contacts, where they're at, who they're connected to, how they drive business, all your deals, every process point, every waypoint and a schedule in your head. Your internal rolodex give you 100% confidence that you know what you need to know. There's no need to put it on paper, or worse – the *cloud* for your manager to review.

Databases are awful because you must maintain them and if you're maintaining your databases, are you closing? Databases suck because they're always changing. Doesn't your company bring in a new CRM every few years? It's ridiculous. Databases are an anchor that weigh you down and create ridiculous conversations between you and your manager about where a prospect is at in **your** pipeline or the weak point in **your** funnel. What about **their** funnel?

Your company has told you that as a salesperson, you run your business like it is your business, so why should you have to fill in *their* database? Can your database point out bottlenecks in their process? Some might say that databases bring transparency and force you into a position of accountability. Why would you want that? You deal with enough rejection and corporate accountability that something like a database is enough to make you throw your arms up and walk away.

Can a database tell you why you have an engagement, timetable, or closing problem? It seems to me that databases expose your problems but don't give you the answer; so who cares? Databases are a hammer; a brutal tool that sales managers use to break you down. Managers use your database to make you feel inadequate and incompetent. Databases are roadblocks and obstacles that prevent you from doing closing.

Can a database reveal the strength of your relationship with the customer? Hardly! Databases are all about dispassionate analysis of the current situation, but you are a passionate salesperson, you don't have time for reality checks because you make your reality. The more information you keep in your head, the better – it's yours. How good would you feel if you have filled out your database and then your sales manager takes an account away from you and transfers it to another person and then that person uses the information you had to make the sale? Pretty lousy, right?

A well-maintained database points out what is right and what is wrong, what is relevant and what is not, where opportunity exists and where it doesn't. Why would you want to give that information to your sales manager? Your knowledge sets you apart.

Disregard your database; then you will be regarded as a shitty salesperson.

WATCH LOTS OF TV

Shitty Nick watched a lot of TV. Don't you work hard? Don't you need to vegg-out? Doesn't your brain need to decompress? Nothing beats the positivity streaming from your nearest screen.

When you wake up in the morning, turn on the TV. When you're in the air, watch movies. When you're on the train, watch the news. When you get into the office, pull up YouTube. When you take a lunch break, go to a bar that has a TV. Have an excuse to get out of the office for a client visit? Anywhere you can swing by that has a 'boob tube,' do it. When you get home, turn on the TV and keep it on all night long. The TV is great because it fills your brain with so much information. You get to know who was murdered and who was raped. You get to know which politician cheated and which business person lied. And that's just fiction!

Watch a lot of sports. When you watch a lot of sports, you will increase your odds of having a sports-related conversation with a prospect. That's where buyers and sellers connect! Build rapport through the happenings of the NBA or NASCAR. You want to be able to talk about the QBR and the RBI, games above 500, playoff implications, trade deadlines and contracts are always a hot topic. You and the prospect will connect on how all these issues bring you immense happiness or suffering because as your sports team goes, so goes your happiness.

Not into sports? *The Kardashians* will give you all the drama you need for a week. Still not satiated? Jump to *Jersey Shore*. Need to cry a lot over nothing? Watch *This is Us*. Need senseless violence disguised in a good story? *Law and Order SVU*. Who doesn't like hearing about a good child rape mystery? *Flip or Flop* is a neat way to skew your perception of reality. E! and Bravo help you see all the dreams you're not personally realizing. If you want non-news disguised as real news, tune into CNN. If you want fake news, watch FOX News. Both will infuriate you or reinforce your echo chamber.

What's the common thread in all of this? None of it will help you sell. You need a break. You need time to decompress. You need to escape the prison that is your job with the slavery that is your fantasy. TV can make you a great water cooler talker. It might create a connection with your secretary. It might provide a light-hearted moment in a sales meeting.

What it won't do, and why would you want it to, is help you understand the customer's motive, empathize with their pain and see hard-to-identify opportunities. The TV won't help you relate, engage, and challenge. The TV doesn't drive creativity, improve relationships, or start genuine conversations. All those things take work – you've got other work to do, like cold call.

Watch as much television as you can, and when it comes to becoming a salesperson, you'll broadcast one shit-show.

FORGET MARKETING

Shitty Nick knows a tough fact about business: "marketing" is for people who can't sell.

Marketing is a business discipline that shouldn't get a minute of your time. Don't engage with your marketing team. Don't try to put ideas in their head about how to market the product. Don't tell them what your customers tell you because Marketers won't understand it. Why? Marketing is an ideas game, not a results game, and you are a results-oriented person.

Marketing is about telling people what something does using lots of bells, whistles, and buzzwords. Marketing is for people who don't have thick skin and can't handle rejection like you. Avoid marketing like you'd avoid The Plague. Pick up your phone, smile, and dial. Hit the bricks, knock on doors, and get people to press hard because there are three copies. That's how to sell. Not engaging content.

Customers don't care about how flashy a packet looks. Can prospects be engaged by a video? Could the survey a prospect takes result in a meaningful conversation? And what about social media marketing... as if people are really interested in seeing pictures of the house you're listing on Instagram, or a fancy infographic on how to leverage insurance policies posted on LinkedIn, or a YouTube video of how your new widget improves employee safety, or reading a blog post on *Medium* that is full of testimonials from your customers about how awesome you are. Nobody cares about that.

When is the last time you did that and it drove an inbound call or landed an email in your inbox with a request to get coffee? Prospects hate marketing in both the business and personal world. It's why you subscribe to Netflix – no commercials! Prospects know what's in the marketplace. They have both a high-level awareness of what's in the marketplace and an acute understanding of differences between products. The result is their innate knowledge about what they should buy.

When is the last time marketing produced a solid inbound lead of someone who was legitimately interested in buying from you? They don't because Marketing isn't interested in generating your leads. Marketing doesn't want your ideas; they don't need your ideas. Marketing is totally uninterested in your ideas. What's marketing want? A paycheck without responsibility.

Here are a few more reasons to stay away from marketing. What do you know about content? Are you an artist or a graphic designer? Do you know anything about those disciplines? If not, what input could you have on how a brochure or a video or a website looks? Could you benefit to learn those things and to understand what might catch a consumer's eye? Are you an English major with lots of copywriting and editing skills, if not, what voice and what right do you have to put any of that out there in the public domain? You're just going to make mistakes, look bad, and perhaps put your company in jeopardy.

Marketing people think they are so damn special and only they can create the silver bullet or the magic concoction that will drive so many inbound leads that you won't have time to make a cold call. Has there ever been a crazier idea in all of sales? Sales happen because people like you pick up the phone, push the pain button, and then offer the cheapest price.

You don't need a flyer or video. You don't need a website or powerPoint deck. You don't need Facebook. You don't need LinkedIn. You don't need a marketing team behind you exploring the prospects fundamental buying issues. You don't need a marketing team to engage emotinally engage probable purchasers. You don't need a marketing lesson on how to grab the buyer's attention. All those theories are nothing but busy work for a made-up profession of people who can't sell.

Forget marketing, and you'll never have to market that you're a shitty salesperson.

TAKE YOURSELF VERY SERIOUSLY

Shitty Nick knew how people viewed him and what they said about him. He could hear them in his head say things like "Wow! Can you believe he just did that? That took some guts!"

Everyone is jealous of the salesperson. Everyone wants to be like you — the aggressive, smooth-talking hunter who creates business out of thin air. When you think about who you are, remember that you are exceedingly important and that what you do every day makes the world go 'round. This isn't arrogance. That's reality, and it doesn't matter if you sell papers, pencils, or prescription drugs.

You are vital to the success of the organization and your community. Just think what might happen to your company if you weren't there... how they would be deprived of such breadth and depth of knowledge and experience! As a salesperson, you stand as the inspiration for the rest of the company, and you have all the symbols to show it. Look at your timepiece, the sports jacket you wear, the purse you carry, the car you drive, the country club you belong to, the accolades you receive. Your list of awards and trophies for excellent production are the envy of the office.

Sales is not a joking matter because life is sales, and life isn't funny. You know who you are as a salesperson. You are the person everyone else wants to be because you are special. You know that people want and need your opinion on every topic. You always have something relevant to say, and people generally love the sound of your voice. The advice you offer is always applicable. The insights you provide are always unique. In your way, as a salesperson, you are CEO.

Your assessment of complex situations is always spot-on. You're a big deal, everybody knows it, and they appreciate it. As the BSD, you command respect and admiration for your successes and failures. If more people acted with the chutzpah you exude, the competition would run and hide.

You're the bulldog and the lynchpin. Whther you're at work, at home, or your kid's soccer game – people know it. You sell. You're a real-life porn star. All other business units are your fluffers. Because when you score, they score.

Don't back down and never be ashamed because a shameless salesperson is a shitty salesperson.

FORGET FOLLOW UP AND IGNORE FOLLOW THROUGH

Shitty Nick worked on a simple philosophy that paid incredible dividends: don't follow-up or follow through. Lots of people like to say: "fortune is in the follow-up and fame is in the follow through." How cute. Fortune is not in the follow-up. You find fortune by delivering the product cheaper than the competition. What's the point in answering 97 follow up question if you don't have the cheapest price?

Most of the time you can get away with doing zero or minimal follow-up and come in at 5 or 10% under the next lowest price and have a serious shot at winning. When is the last time you heard a customer say they wanted a complete solution that met all their needs? My experience shows that if you can give someone 85% of what they want for 60% of the price, they are going to take that over 100% of what they want for 100% of the price. Included in that discount is your lack of follow up.

This fact destroys any validity of relationship, solution, or challenger sales. Find people who are interested in doing one thing more than any other, saving money. Everyone wants a deal because when they get a deal, they feel like they've won. They feel like they've beat you. Well, let them beat you so you can beat the competition. Who cares if the solution is ultimately inadequate? It's the buyer's job to be aware. Is it your job to help them be aware? Hard not to laugh, right?

Look at your business card. It says, Salesperson. It doesn't say, helper. Why would you bother sending a thank you letter after a meeting? Will that help you get another meeting? Does it help you get a new prospect? No, it takes up your time and it might give the customer the feeling that you aren't desperate. They want to buy from a desperate salesperson because desparate = discount. You must make money, so whatever.

What about following up to questions from the sales meeting? Simple rule: prospects only care if they ask the same question three times. Every minute following-up is a minute not cold calling your next new customer. The only reason managers want to see follow up is because they think they are overpaying you for the job you're doing. They want to see 20 contacts before the sale closes. It's a giant waste of your time.

Customers don't care that you are reliable. They don't care that they can call you up and you will get back to them as soon as possible with an honest answer. They're ok not being a priority. They're not worried about their time. They care about spending the least amount of money as possible to take away the pain. The rest is noise. Following up and following through are just code words for "more work for you, less money per hour." Your goal is to do as little work for as much as possible. Not as much work for as much as possible.

Don't waste your time with following-up or following-through and you will never have to answer a follow-up question about why you are a shitty salesperson.

ABANDON ATTITUDE

Shitty Nick will tell you: All this attitude talk from "sales gurus" is nothing but a jar of snake oil. What's the most absurd quack remedy they try to sell you? The power of *attitude.*

Take this challenge: define attitude. Is it your feelings? Is it your thoughts? Is it a combination? Is it how you approach a problem? Yes? No? All the above? It's impossible to describe. If you can't talk about it or describe it, isn't it ridiculous to try and preach about it?

Second, what is a good attitude? And for that matter, what is a bad attitude? Is a good attitude for one person the same as a good attitude for another person? Is attitude black and white? Is it universal? And how do you know if you have it? Once you have it, do you always have it? Can you lose it? Can you make it better? A conundrum, and that's the point.

What is the point of talking about something when you can't accurately describe it and when you can't equally apply it to everyone in all situations? Perhaps, the biggest question is: is a good attitude something you can possess? Is it something you can learn? Is it something you can develop? Who knows? But it seems to be a sellable topic, at least according to all these sales experts, and you've bought it, haven't you?

These people talk about how attitude drives thoughts, emotions, actions; how attitude helps you see problems from different perspectives, engage difficult people, and overcome serious objections. They sure think it can - or at least they can write about it to sell books. But does attitude help you? When's the last time you turned attitude into cash?

Does improving your attitude make you a better person or more importantly, a better salesperson? Is part of your attitude figured into your annual bonus or your commission schedule? If not, why should you care? Can your confidence or lack thereof impact the outcome of a situation? Can it change other people's perspective of you or your product or service? Can it set you apart from the rest of the sales pack? Hell if I know. I've never paid any attention to it.

You don't need attitude. You need a phone, to smile and dial. You need the guts to ask for the sale no matter the customer's circumstances. You don't need a healthy attitude. The only attitude you need is the one that says you are God's gift to the customer and your company. People should get out of your way so you can do the job they're unwilling to do, and they should be grateful for your efforts no matter what they produce.

Isn't that the attitude that counts? And if it is, that's the attitude of a shitty salesperson.

IGNORE SELF REFLECTION

Shitty Nick never thought about his actions or associated them with his paycheck. There's no time. Like you, Shitty Nick had a quota to meet. Self-improvement is a myth and the only thing that matters in sales is numbers. The problem with self-reflection is you can't change who you are.

Be like Shitty Nick and look for the shortcut. Train yourself to focus on profit. Embraced a "screw you!" attitude. Isn't that who you are? Does the customer care what kind of a person you are? Does the customer care that you've grown and developed highly-skilled sales strategies and tactics? Does the customer care if you asked yourself if what you are doing is good for everyone? No way. Customers care about relieving pain and price, not your well-being.

Do you think that customers care if you have found a better way to engage them, speak their language, or see things from their perspective? What's the point? Customer preferences change from one day to the next and from one customer to the next. You trying to better yourself is an exercise in futility because nobody cares if you're good or bad. Nobody cares if you are improving. Nobody cares if you're developing as a professional or a person. So why reflect?

Self-reflection will only point out the deficiencies and problems you already know you have. Self-reflection takes away time from cold calling, writing proposals, and sending emails. Those are the activities your manager will grade. How many managers have cared that grew as a professional or as a person under their tutelage? Your development is not their concern, you beating quota is their *only* concern.

Ignore self-reflection so when you look in the mirror, you'll see someone like Nick, a shitty salesperson.

FORGET FAIR

Shitty Nick knew that *fair* is a term thrown out by people who can't sell and an excuse to make up for missed quotas and superior competition.

If being fair gives you less of a chance to win, why would you consider it? If you ain't cheat'n, you ain't try'n. Sales is hard enough as it is. Now someone will tell you that you should always play fair? Easy for them to say when they don't have your quota.

Fair is a relative term. Fair means to be respectful of internal and external competition. Isn't that a different way of saying giving someone else a better chance to beat you? What is wrong with cheating? Who is anyone else to decide? Does fair mean to tell your customer to look at a couple of different solutions or products? Does fair require you to be transparent with pricing and terms? Remember: it's the customer's job to be aware, not your job to help them be aware.

Being fair requires you to think about ethics, morals, and reasonableness - as if a top-selling salesperson can ever stay on the top and retain the moral high ground. Sales is like love and war. All is fair, which means that NOTHING IS FAIR. Don't worry about whether you're doing right by your customer, company, or even yourself. You're getting the sale. Does your manager care how? Not if their bonus relies on it.

Forget fair, and it's fair to say you'll be a fairly shitty salesperson.

DO SHITTY PRODUCT DEMONSTRATIONS

Shitty Nick knew he didn't have to be Billy Mays. Do you? Do you believe customers want to see your product in action before they buy it? Don't you have marketing material and product specs? Can't prospects figure out how to work the widget? Don't you think that they should? But they can't because prospects are dumb, so you've got to do it yourself. If you can convince a customer that your product will work, there's no need to show them that it does work.

Here's are the ultimate mistakes to make a sales presentation shitty.

1) Don't know your product inside and out. You don't have the time to learn all the features and benefits of your product. That's the point of *product people.* That's the domain of Marketing. As a last-ditch out, hopefully, you've got sales engineers. You are the big picture person, the problem solver, the relationship lady. You only need to know what it does, not how it does it. And of course, you always say it does more than it really can. Let the customer figure out the limitations – it's your job to focus on the possibilities!

2) Never rehearse. You have cold calls to make, emails to send and RFPs that need a canned response. You don't have time to practice your presentation. Isn't it better to not know what problems could arise in a presentation, so then you get to throw out the great line of "This is unexpected, let me get back to you with a few workarounds" Haven't you found out how much prospects appreciate it when you tell them you'll "follow-up and get back to them?"

3) Never script a problem you can solve. You don't want customers to see a problem. Why in the world would they want to see you solve a problem? They expect things to work perfectly, but since you don't have the time or inclination to make it perfect, why would you even consider high-

lighting or acting out a problem? If you are presenting with another person, dominate the conversation.

4) Don't lay out a plan where the customer's problem is solved. What if you risk not being 100% right or 100% applicable? They don't think you're going to be a perfect fit anyway, so why try to be one? You want them to think that you might have the solution. What's the rush in getting them excited and signing today? What if you need to sandbag? You want to do just enough for them to be interested but not take action.

5) Don't bother memorizing the answers to the top 20 frequently asked questions. There is no guarantee someone will even ask these questions, so why worry about the answers? Never ask for feedback on features and benefits as that opens the door to the customer sharing something that they don't like.

6) Never demonstrate how the customer benefits. They're will make their judgments. Is it your job to show them how they win? Of course not. You can't know their business or industry as well as your customer, so why try? Your job is to show them how the product works and how much it costs. They decide if it's good or not for them.

Product demonstrations are a necessary evil, but if you can routinely put out half-assed performances, you'll do a great job performing as a shitty salesperson.

IGNORE THE GOLDEN RULE

Shitty Nick lives the *Golden Rule*: "Do unto others as you'd have them do unto you." You do things one way, so people return the favor. But never be deceived by the *original* rule: "*As you do unto others, you do unto yourself*." Whoa! That's not how salespeople are supposed to sell.

Sales is about getting people to do what you want them to do. Does it matter how you get them to do it? No. Sales is the best example of the ends justifying the means, and this gives you the incredible latitude with your behavior towards other people.

Just think what would happen if you had to apply the *original meaning* of the Golden Rule to every sales situation. If you give the best deal to your customer, does that mean it's the best deal for you? Probably not. If you offer the most favorable terms to the customer, what is the net result to you and your company? More work. How in the world can you maximize profitability if you're concerned with whether you are cheating the customer and thereby cheating yourself?

Do you expect the customer to reciprocate your behavior? What is the last time a customer has refused a discount, been honest about a pricing mistake, or highlighted the precarious position you or your company is in because of the terms of the contract? Never. If they're not going to do it to you, why in the world should you do it to them?

If you live by the real Golden Rule, it means you might have to tell a customer you're not the best solution and point them in the direction of a competitor. As if anyone would ever say, "If I can help you, I'll tell you, and if I can't I'll help you find someone who will." How pleased would your manager be if you put that in the database? Is that going to get you a bonus... let alone a commission?!

There is only one real Golden Rule in sales, and that is: "Treat others as you need to treat them, and they treat you like they'd treat any other shitty salesperson."

SHITTY PEOPLE

Not only was Nick Shitty, but he also hung around shitty people. They were the true sales warhorses; the reps who've seen and done it all. They know all the tricks customers pull, the lies management tells, and the daggers support staff throws.

Bad attitudes, ideas, and actions are toxic. The more you expose yourself to these events, the more you will successfully hamstring your career. It's cathartic to whine and bitch about customers, coworkers, and managers. Doesn't it feel good to let loose with all your unfiltered and incomplete thoughts and criticisms about other people? There's a lot of work involved, but it's worth it.

If you feel up to the challenge, make sure you hang around shitty people at the right time and in the right place. Bitching with a coworker before a meeting can impact the result of the meeting. It is a great way to poison the well. You can say the same for customers. If you whine about how much they screwed up the implementation or complain about how little money you're getting for all the effort you put in, you will successfully close the door to future opportunities, and then you don't have to work with them anymore.

Make time to meet-up with coworkers at the water cooler/ break room to listen for and spread gossip. They say "timing is everything" so try to time your shit-talking after intense moments of good or bad news. Seek out people who love to talk negatively about coworkers. Birds of a feather stick together; misery loves company.

The best place to hang around negative people is the bar (sidebar: I'm editing this at the bar). Never the chance to make happy hour unhappy by complaining over a beer. With the loose tongues that arrive after several libations, you will go to dark places. Criticisms of your coworkers and customers will be sharper and resonate with your coworkers.

Don’t you appreciate the saying “garbage in garbage out?” Try as you might you can't make shit shine. Embrace the freedom of expression. Don't co-mingle with coworkers, commiserate. Sow the seeds of discord throughout your organization by focusing on your works and shortcomings.

Find people who are never happy, who love to complain, and never offer legitimate solutions. Feed them your negativity and feed off theirs. Exaggerate experiences and highlight their pain to coworkers. Tell them that “you understand” and that their “feelings are justified.” Never challenge preconceived notions. Mix negativity with positivy and watch the sparks fly!

Be the realist that people appreciate you for and hang around the so-called naysayers. People will be grateful for your honesty, and you can veil it in the cloth of candor. There is no virtue in hanging around a Polly Anna. The beauty of dragging other people down and being dragged down by other people is that it quickly evens the playing field.

Hang with shitty salespeople, and you’ll be a shitty salesperson.

TINDER SALES

You don't have time to strategically think about who you're talking to, what their interests are, the common ground you share, and the place your minds can meet so business can happen. You need to *Tinder Sales.*

Substantive relationships are a myth. What's not a myth? Making as many calls and as many stops as you possibly can in a given day. Just like making as many *swipe lefts* in a day. That's what gets business and that's what gets you dates. You don't need to go in armed with information, just go in with the blind belief that no matter what, you can help and are a catch.

Do you really think a new prospect would care that you know their name or came in with a recommendation from someone else, or with a lead for their business? No way! They're expecting you to be ignorant so play that card every single time. They're ignorant, you're ignorant and ignorance is bliss.

How do you *Tinder Sales?* Ask these opening questions (either in-person or over the phone):

"Are you the owner or manager?" *Tinder Sales: Are you single-ish?*
-This question is great because it tells people you're there to talk to a decision-maker and that you're important enough to interrupt their day

"Are you the person that makes decisions about X?"
Tinder Sales - are you open to a date?

-You're simply curious, not assuming anything; they'll be happy to open up and tell you what you need to know

"When's the last time you changed your widget?" *Tinder Sales - I'm horny, how 'bout you?*
-An easy question to ask because people always know the answer

If people don't respond the way you want them to, swipe left!

Don't waste your time learning about how the business interacts with the community. Nobody wants to talk about what they've done to make life better in the neighborhood. They're interested in making money, you're interested in making money, isn't that enough? They want affection, you give affection, it works!

If you knock on doors, don't plan out your first 10 stops the previous night. Anything can happen between 430PM and 9AM so why bother knowing if the owner or manager is in? And is it your concern if you walk in when a business is likely busy? No! Just like viewing pictures, you churn through until you see something you like and then take your shot.

You don't need information, you need five minutes, or the first meeting, or an Email address. Once you have those things, the rest of the sale is elementary! Prospects doesn't care if you understand their needs. Nor do they care if you're tuned-in with their customer's customer. Who's business are you trying to help?

That's why developing a calling strategy is pointless. Efficiency isn't your concern – that's not what you're graded on. You're graded on the number of calls and the number of closes. Your boss wants to see you make 60 stops or 100 calls in a day because they believe that's what's necessary to get two meetings. So why try to have a meeting conversion rate of 25% when that would take away from your overall number of calls?

Shitty Nick did *Tinder Sales* before Tinder existed. In practice, Shitty Nick did one thing better than most other sales people: he prospected with such blind aggression that from the moment he said "hello" until he walked out the door, people knew he was a shitty salesperson. The same happened in his dating life - now married with kids, he's an inspiration!

DON'T FINISH

Shitty Nick started his career in sales – he's still there. Unable or unwilling to move beyond, this book acts as a memoir and guide to those people who want to emulate his behavior and experience his success.

What are the results of *not* finishing? You procrastinate and doubt. You juxtapose urgent with important. You become afraid of what success or even completion might mean to you and how others perceive you.

There's a finality when completion happens that can be used to judge, mock, and ridicule you for how you think, feel, and write. But if you never finish, those critiques won't happen. By not finishing, you never face rejection.

By not finishing, you remove the major component of self-reflection. Nobody can judge what you don't finish. It's hard to reward and even harder to punish when you don't finish. Excuses pop up.

If you don't finish, you won't worry about setting a standard by which you should improve. Life is easy for those who don't finish. Lessons can't be fully learned, absorbed, and applied. It builds your Excuse Machine for doing the same thing over and over and expecting different results.

Not finishing allows you to push blame elsewhere, on circumstances outside of your control and onto customers who only care about their problems or on managers who aren't supportive. The shitty salesperson never finishes. They remain perpetually three feet from gold. They don't have time to grow beyond who and what they are because they have a cold call to make, a proposal to respond to, and to price to quote.

A shitty salesperson never finishes making excuses. A shitty salesperson never finishes blaming others. A shitty salesperson never finishes leaving success at the doorstep of another. If you want to be a shitty salesperson, this book is the blueprint. Make it your new Sales Gospel.

Let the close go. Let the customer do whatever they want to. Your help is transactional, not transformational. Don't be the difference. Don't be the catalyst. Don't open the Doors of Opportunity.

You can't make a difference so stop trying to do more than the bare minimum. Do as little as you can to keep your paycheck. Never finish being more than mediocre. Never stop living safely. Don't try the great experiment of greatness; you can't finish it.

Here's the best part: by reading this book you'll have a lifetime of behaviors and excuses you can use to place blame. This is your guide to abdicate responsibility. You can take what's written and make it real. Follow the examples, embrace these attitudes, thoughts, and behaviors.

The result?, You've got a new excuse - you can blame it all on me: this book from the world's shittiest salesperson.

BACK-WORD

Hi Customer.

Despite the absolute ridiculousness of this book, if your salesperson gave it to you, they're serious about two things: earning your business and **not** being a shitty salesperson.

This book is a tool to keep the salesperson accountable. Because you, *the buyer,* have rights. You have expectations salespeople should meet – but often fail to do so. Salespeople are under intense pressure to perform, and the incentives for performing (and punishments for failing) are immense. The result? Shitty behavior.

Have you ever made the wrong decision because you had to deal with a shitty salesperson? Have you ever bought something you shouldn't or not bought something you should? That's not right or fair! This book aims to put a stop to those painful events.

Your salesperson read this book and identified five of their biggest deficiencies. By putting these ideas down on paper, it's easier for both of you to identify and rectify any problem. You shouldn't make the wrong decision because the salesperson is shitty.

1) ______________________________
2) ______________________________
3) ______________________________
4) ______________________________
5) ______________________________

I'm not saying that if a salesperson gives you this book, you should buy from them. But you should appreciate someone who is willing to talk about their shortcomings. The self-aware salesperson is likelier to ask tough questions about their behavior and motivations. That salesperson is open to exploring (and ultimately changing) their behaviors. Isn't that a breath of fresh air compared to most of the other (willfully) ignorant salespeople who are only interested in your signature?

Don't most salespeople try to start from a position of strength? If your salesperson gave you this book, there's a willingness to start from a position of weakness and as weird as it sounds, salespeople who aren't afraid of their deficiencies are the most likely to embrace the best sales attitude I've ever heard. It's from Jeffrey Gitomer. He tells probable purchaser the following statement early-on in the relationship – he means it, he acts it, and people appreciate it: "Let's talk over lunch, get to know one another a bit, and if I believe I can help you, I'll tell you. And if I don't believe I can help you, I'll tell you that too – and help you find someone who can."

Wouldn't that be great to hear on the phone, or at a networking event, or in an Email? They said it – hold them to their word and you're likelier to have a better experience.

You get 37 solicitations a day. Who would you rather work with? The salesperson who isn't afraid of their warts or the one who demands you worship them? It's not your responsibility to make the salesperson better. But aren't the potential emotional and financial rewards worth a hard conversation?

This book is your tool to build a great relationship with your salesperson. You don't need to buy from them because of this book, but your experience with them should be healthier than average and certainly more functional. This book is your way to "right the ship," so you don't miss out on a great opportunity because they were a shitty salesperson.

Above all, this book is your way to help a salesperson help you make the best decision for your business. Hold their feet to the fire and profit in the process — a true, win-win.

Made in the USA
San Bernardino, CA
26 February 2019